PENGUIN BOOKS

FIRSTLIGHT

Sue Monk Kidd is the award-winning author of two bestselling novels, *The Secret Life of Bees* and *The Mermaid Chair*, as well as three highly acclaimed spiritual memoirs, *God's Joyful Surprise*, *When the Heart Waits*, and *The Dance of the Dissident Daughter*. She lives near Charleston, South Carolina, with her husband, Sandy, and their black lab, Lily. She writes in a book-lined study where she can look out at the tidal creeks and marsh birds. She is at work on a new book.

fIRSTLIGHT

THE EARLY INSPIRATIONAL WRITINGS
OF
SUE MONK KIDD

PENGUIN BOOKS

PENGUIN BOOKS

Published by the Penguin Group
Penguin Group (USA) Inc., 375 Hudson Street, New York, New York 10014, U.S.A.
Penguin Group (Canada), 90 Eglinton Avenue East, Suite 700, Toronto,
Ontario, Canada M4P 2Y3 (a division of Pearson Penguin Canada Inc.)
Penguin Books Ltd, 80 Strand, London WC2R 0RL, England
Penguin Ireland, 25 St Stephen's Green, Dublin 2, Ireland (a division of Penguin Books Ltd)
Penguin Group (Australia), 250 Camberwell Road, Camberwell,
Victoria 3124, Australia (a division of Pearson Australia Group Pty Ltd)
Penguin Books India Pvt Ltd, 11 Community Centre,
Panchsheel Park, New Delhi – 110 017, India
Penguin Group (NZ), 67 Apollo Drive, Rosedale, North Shore 0745,
Auckland, New Zealand (a division of Pearson New Zealand Ltd)
Penguin Books (South Africa) (Pty) Ltd, 24 Sturdee Avenue,
Rosebank, Johannesburg 2196, South Africa

Penguin Books Ltd, Registered Offices:
80 Strand, London WC2R 0RL, England

First published in the United States of America by GuidepostsBooks 2006
Published in Penguin Books 2007

1 3 5 7 9 10 8 6 4 2

Copyright © GuidepostsBooks, 2006
All rights reserved

Please see page 229 for acknowledgments.

THE LIBRARY OF CONGRESS HAS CATALOGED THE HARDCOVER EDITION AS FOLLOWS:
Kidd, Sue Monk.
Firstlight : early inspirational writings / Sue Monk Kidd.
p. cm.
ISBN 0-8249-4706-1 (hc.)
ISBN 978-0-14-311232-7 (pbk.)
1. Christian life.   I. Title.
BV4515.3.K53 2006
242—dc22   2006006989

Printed in the United States of America
Designed by Marisa Jackson

FOR MY PARENTS, LEAH AND RIDLEY MONK,
MY MOTHER-IN-LAW, LAVERNE KIDD,
AND IN MEMORY OF MY FATHER-IN-LAW,
MAXEY KIDD,
WITH ABIDING LOVE.

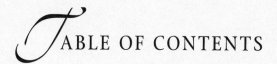

TABLE OF CONTENTS

INTRODUCTION

WHEN GUIDEPOSTSBOOKS first approached me about collecting my early inspirational writings into one volume, I was ambivalent. I had no idea then what a remarkable gift this book would become for me. I was only imagining how humbling it could be to read my work from those first, developmental years. What fifty-seven-year-old writer wants to go back and read what she wrote when she was thirty years old? I imagined it would be a little like looking at old photographs of myself in a forgotten album and being appalled at my hairstyles, wondering why I'd chosen a bouffant or why bell-bottoms had seemed like a good idea. I thought about the stories and meditations I'd composed all those years ago on a portable typewriter in a corner of the family den as I jumped up every five minutes to tend to my toddlers. Would I read them and wince at certain sentences or wonder why I'd thought it was a good idea to write about the death of my daughter's goldfish or an encounter with an old woman on a sand dune?

What is it about revealing one's beginnings that is so disconcerting? Is it because our beginnings contain so many "bad hairdos"? It seemed likely that the writing I'd done in my literary pubescence would possess a natural greenness—less maturity in my voice, technique, style, and language. More disconcerting than that, however, was that my early work was autobiographical in nature and *spiritual* to boot. As my writing had evolved, so had I. My spirituality had moved through long and laborious courses, growing deeper and more permeable, increasingly able to hold uncertainties, ambiguities, unorthodoxies, and was marked by a rich and restless searching. Did I want to revisit what seemed like less seasoned times? Would there be too much piety in those early efforts?

For as long as I can remember I've been compelled to write about the workings of my soul, to record my ponderings about God and my search for meaning in things great and minuscule. "I cannot see my soul, but know 'tis there," wrote Emily

Dickinson. Some part of me has always felt the truth of that, has experienced moments of quickening when the knowledge of a mysterious, unseen inner life flames up. Meister Eckhart, a theologian from centuries back, called this combustion the "god-spark." Thomas Merton, the well-known Trappist monk, referred to God's presence in the soul as the *pointe vierge*. This French phrase refers to the "virgin point" that comes just before dawn, those ripening moments before the first ray of light flares into the darkness. Whatever name we give this hidden incandescence, this "firstlight," I believe it exists in all of us. I believe, too, in the impulse to capture its flickerings through words. It seems that I'd been trying to do this in one way or another, with varying degrees of skill, experience, and success from the moment I set upon the writing life.

Arguably, a significant portion of my life can be understood as a spiritual quest and the articulation of that experience. I'd written dozens of stories, personal essays, meditations, and inspirational reflections during the inaugural decade. They'd all had their brief lives—a small flourishing— then disappeared beneath the layers of years. I'd had no desire to dig them up.

It was eye-opening, finally, to see that my ambivalence over having my earliest writings excavated and republished in the present came from a well-meaning conceit: I wanted to be read and known for who I am *now*.

Naturally, the moment I came to this, paradox reared its head. What if knowing who I am now is incomplete without knowing who I was then? What if part of me was lost back there with that body of work? Did I have to return to the place of my origins as a writer in order to understand myself fully? Can we ever go forward without going backward?

At some point, while nesting in this tangle of questions, I recalled something I'd read about Merton. First, I suppose you should know that Merton's writings were perhaps the most formative works I've ever read. His famous autobiographical book, *The Seven Storey Mountain*, written when he was a young man, had a life-altering effect on me when I read it at the age of twenty-nine, a few months before I decided to give myself over to writing. The book revealed to me the startling reality of the inner life, cracking open a raw longing for the Divine and exposing an irrepressible hunger for that deepest thing in myself.

So imagine my bemusement when I read that later in his life Merton had a somewhat ambivalent relationship to *The Seven Storey Mountain*. Apparently he felt it had created a myopic view of him. He had become heavily identified with the Merton in those pages, the pious young monk. He seemed to chafe at the thought of being frozen in those early years—as if they defined, described, and contained the whole of him.

This awareness put me in the unlikely position of experiencing the truth of both sides of this odd dilemma. I knew the power of Merton's first work—I could not imagine *The Seven Storey Mountain* not being part of his canon or not being available in the world—and at the same time, I could relate in my own small way to his brooding tension with it. My early inspirational writing in no way parallels Merton's first masterpiece, but the moment I stood in the middle of this paradox, I was able to open my arms to my thirty-year-old self, to the words that sprang from her portable typewriter in a corner of the den.

Opening myself to the creation of this book, so aptly titled *Firstlight*, became an unexpected act of reclamation.

The surprise to me in all of this was that *Firstlight* became a bridge—a way for me to return to my beginnings, to works that had been lost, orphaned, forgotten and dismissed. It was a gift of reunion.

❧

ON MY THIRTIETH BIRTHDAY, I walked into the kitchen of my brick house in South Carolina and announced to my husband and two children, "I'm going to become a writer." That was my annunciation. In a kitchen. To a two-year-old and a five-year-old and a husband who was trying to get them to eat their cereal. My plan was earnest but highly unlikely. I lovingly refer to it now as my "great absurdity." We should all have one or two of those in our lives—a hope so extravagant it seems completely foolish and implausible. I'd studied nursing and worked during my twenties in hospitals on surgical, pediatric and obstetrical units, even spending one summer as a public health nurse. I didn't know anything about creative writing or whether I had any ability for it. All I had was the impulse and passion of my heart.

It was during the months prior to turning thirty that my

creative life began to wake up. I had the feeling of something urgent and necessary pressing in, wanting to be born. I think it had a lot to do with reading the aforementioned book by Merton and discovering the deep place within where I was sourced—the interior realm of the soul. My creativity seems to emanate from making portals into this inscrutable land. For me, creativity is essentially a spiritual experience, a conversation between my soul and me. So it's probably not coincidental that my writing life began almost simultaneously with my initiating this conversation.

The day after my birthday, I enrolled in a writing class in which the teacher gave us an assignment: Write a personal experience article and send it off to a magazine. I wrote a very simple story about the first Thanksgiving after I was married and submitted it to a writing contest sponsored by a magazine that I'd often seen lying about the house when I was growing up. The magazine was *Guideposts*, an inter-faith, inspirational publication with millions of subscribers, which had been founded by the late Dr. Norman Vincent Peale and his wife, Ruth Stafford Peale, in 1945. To my amazement, I was one of fifteen winners who were invited to New York to a writers' workshop. You can ask anyone who was there and they'll tell you I barely opened my mouth the entire time. I believe the Guideposts staff assumed I was shy, but the truth was I felt like I'd been dropped off on a new and unknown planet. People spoke a mysterious literary lingo—*in medias res*, SASEs, take-aways, *denouements*. I'm pretty sure I was the only writer there who could not speak the language, who'd never had anything published, and whose whole assemblage of work was comprised of one story. Mostly, though, mine was the silence of a sponge soaking up everything.

That was 1978. I would continue writing for *Guideposts* for the next twelve years.

It was through *Guideposts* that I began an apprenticeship to the narrative form. I learned not only how to write stories, but to love them, to revere them even. I discovered the power of honest, personal, revelatory writing. Humans, I discovered, need stories the way we need air.

❦

THE MAJORITY OF WRITINGS in this book come from the work I did for *Guideposts* during those dozen years. When the publisher sent me the stack of work that had been compiled for this book, I was astonished at the assortment, the wide medley of variation. I discovered my first published piece in the pile—a story about an unusual experience I'd had with death and forgiveness while working as a nurse during my early twenties. (You will find it in the last chapter.) There were, in fact, several stories from the few years I'd spent as a nurse, as well as a plethora of stories about my mothering years, about my children (who now have children of their own). I discovered my recollections about the year I lived in Africa, meditations on my childhood and my grandparents, reflections on my marriage and on a stream of common moments: watching a bird feeder, a homeless man, a golf tournament. There were numerous chronicles about travels to the shore and to the mountains, as well as to the Chalice Well garden in England and to Gethsemane garden in Israel. I read articles I'd written about moments of crisis and transition, and short devotionals—anecdotes from which I'd extrapolated a message.

Material from other sources exist here as well, notably a series of longer essays published in *Weavings: A Journal of the*

Christian Spiritual Life, written in my forties, which contain more complex renderings of my spiritual experience.

The works in this collection are not arranged chronologically, but gathered loosely around thirteen motifs. You'll find an essay I wrote for *Weavings* in 1995 followed by a *Daily Guideposts* devotional I wrote in 1983, both of them about solitude.

In order to adapt the writings for the book, I made minimal edits, primarily in the form of tightening sentences, clarifying an insight, or adding a few words here and there, but otherwise the pieces remain unchanged.

Perhaps it goes without saying that the collection does not comprise a whole portrait of my life during that time, but rather offers bits and pieces of it. Nevertheless, I'm the first to admit there's a revelation of myself going on here. At the core of personal spiritual writing is a hungering for wholeness, for self, for meaning. The question "Who am I?" reverberates quietly in these pages, as does a willingness to be known. I wonder sometimes why I chose to make my spiritual musings visible. I want to believe it is mostly because such vulnerability creates what we might call "a soulful being together" between the reader and the author. A kind of communion born through the meeting of vulnerability and identification. It is in this delicate communion that books bestow their small transformations.

❦

I HAVE COME TO LOVE the following words by the French Nobel laureate, Albert Camus: "A person's life purpose is nothing more than to rediscover, through the detours of art, or love, or passionate work, those one or two images in the presence of which his heart first opened."

Where did your heart first open? And how shall you find your way back to that dawning?

My hope is that this book—*Firstlight*—will, in its modest way, help to point you there. To the place of your beginning. To the moments when the light broke and your heart opened.

THE CRUCIBLE OF STORY

IT WAS ALMOST CHRISTMAS. I scurried up a ladder to decorate the mantle with cedar. As I arrived at the top rung, my chest began to throb with pain. An hour later I was attached to an electrocardiograph, watching the squiggly lines and trying to figure out how such an incomprehensible thing could happen. "The chest pains seem to be stress-related," the doctor said. I winced at the words.

Now I would have to think about my life. About the disorienting speed at which I lived, the overload of activities. I would have to figure out why I could not say "no," why my days seemed like the squiggly lines on that scrolling paper. Thinking brought a familiar ache of emptiness, the hunger that was always there beneath my busyness, the obscure longing for something I could not name.

I went home from the hospital baffled and afraid. My life seemed suddenly unpinned. It was coming apart. In desperation I opened my Bible. I read until I came to the passage about the lame and sick who lay among the porticoes at the pool of Bethesda. "For an angel went down at a certain season into the pool, and troubled the water: whosoever then first after the troubling of the water stepped in was made whole . . ."

The image touched me in a profound way. I wondered if the water of Bethesda was a mystery that was happening inside me. Who was the angel that disturbed the water of my soul? Was I being asked to step down into my own troubled depths?

I had been lying on the porticoes of my life for years. Now I had come upon "a certain season," some holy moment when I must wade into the empty hunger that swirled beneath the surface of my life. I knew there would be no wholeness unless I stepped down into my darkness and confronted the troubling angel within.

For weeks I sat in an agony of stillness. I reflected and prayed. I went away for solitary retreats. I peeled open my soul and met my troubling angel.

She was the perfectionist who dwelled in me, a relentless

achiever who won love and approval by doing and performing. She insisted that I define myself around the herculean roles and agendas that made up my life. "If you want to be loved, make yourself lovable," she told me. "You are valued by what you do, not who you are." At times her voice took on the piety of Scripture. "Be ye therefore perfect even as your Father which is in heaven is perfect." I recognized her everywhere in time and memory: the times I forced myself to accept another job at church, the times I went to great lengths to please others and most of all to please God. In my head I knew about the divine love I did not have to earn. But in my heart I had no knowledge of it at all. Now, broken by my drivenness, reduced to blue tranquilizers to get through the day, I saw that beneath my frantic doing I was starving for the immediacy of God's love, for a presence I had been too busy to cultivate.

Confronting the troubling angel in the waters of my soul began my journey toward wholeness, a journey that carried me into the fierce tenderness of God's love. Through solitude and silence I began to find an inner music, a love song being sung in the spaces of my own heart. In the mystery of contemplative prayer I learned to enter God's presence within and experience myself loved beyond reason. Slowly my per-fectionist, relieved of her desperate need for love and approval, was transformed.

The pain I experienced on the ladder at Christmas became the sacred hinge of my life, a pivotal experience. I climbed down from the ladder into a new way of being and relating to God. I found that I could not climb my way up to God in a blaze of doing and performing. Rather, I had to descend into the depths of myself and find God there in the darkness of troubled waters. That is the story of how I came dripping-new into the spiritual life.

DISCOVERING OUR PERSONAL STORIES is a spiritual quest. Without such stories we cannot be fully human, for without them we are unable to articulate or even understand our deepest experiences.

Many of us left the storied approach to life at our nursery windows and crossed the threshold into adulthood to more log-ical, didactic ways of making sense of the world. In a culture that is rational, scientific, and abstract we have lost touch with the intuitive, imaginative, and concrete dimensions that inform story. And as the church has made theology and doctrine the core of our religious expression, we have become unstoried in the spiritual life as well. We have lost the ability to probe the soul, to know and refine its experiences.

Once I asked people in a small group to tell a story from their spiritual journeys. Many people told not stories, but gave professions of what they believed—dogmas and propositions. Exiled from their stories and from forums where stories are told, these people had lost the narrative edge of their spiritual existence. They could no longer draw on the power of metaphors, symbols, and inner parables to express their faith. Those who fail to tend to their inner stories risk creating a rift between what they believe and how they live.

As I have worked with my own inner story and helped others do the same, I have seen a conversion take place in several ways.

First, the inner story creates identity, transforming our vision of who we are. Creating story is an act of self-knowing. Through the lens of story we see the mystery of ourselves more clearly. Knowing who I am hinges on remembering who I have been in the past and embracing the hope of who I may be in the future. Story allows me to enter the tension between memory and hope.

When we enter our personal story, we embark on an odyssey of reconciliation, of reclaiming more of who we truly are, the selves that are dark and light, redeemed and unredeemed.

The self-awareness I gained through the story of my inner perfectionist enabled me to begin the work of transformation. The climactic moment came during a retreat at the monastery of St. Meinrad as I struggled with my pattern of creating identity based on what I accomplished and achieved. I came to know experientially that I am simply God's beloved child and that my true selfhood depends on nothing else.

A second way in which the inner story converts and transforms is by sustaining us in the midst of suffering. I have often seen a story become a holy container in which an individual confronts and overcomes pain and fear.

My experience with chest pains and encountering the raw absence of God at my center was a time of intense darkness and fragility for me. But as I began to form the story—pondering it, writing it, telling it—I found the story supporting me like a pair of arms. The very process of kneading the events into meaning became a ritual of nourishment. My story became bread through which God mediated grace.

I once met a woman who had endured a bitter experience as a homeless person on the streets. Over and over she told me the story. Each time she relived it, she was enabled to come to terms with the pain buried there, to accept and own it. To fashion an inner story of our pain carries us into the heart of it, which is where rebirth inevitably occurs. Telling our story puts us in an inner room with our suffering and allows us to dialogue with it. We begin to see our difficulty in a new context and thereby find the comfort and courage to live it.

Thirdly, the inner tale transforms by reorienting us to new truth and insight, breaking open the hidden holy that dwells in our experience. The word *story* actually means "to know." In the act of creating story there is always an event of coming to know. God surprises us with glimpses and truths we did not grasp until we tried to tell the story. As we shape the experience, an "aha!" emerges, a revelation.

Unearthing my story revealed truth upon truth. It led me from chest pain and stress, to a pattern of drivenness, to an attitude of perfectionism, to a stark hunger of the soul. In the end, the story led me to the immense heart of God.

Discovering my inner story reveals God in time and place, *my* time and place. It sharpens God's voice in the common places where it often goes unnoticed—between the lines of life, so to speak. Through story we draw connections between the happenings of life and the lessons of God. We catch God suddenly in the thick of our days, disclosures unraveling out of the mundane. Such awareness transforms life from a series of random events to the poetic realm of a sacred tale.

When we share our inner stories, we allow others to enter our lives and partake of our deepest truths. We discover that we share the same joys and tragedies, the same ambiguities and struggles. In the end we are all one story. My own tale of the troubling angel repeats in hearts everywhere. For who has not come upon a season when the water of the soul is disturbed? And does not God meet each of us as we brave the swirling dark in search of wholeness?

God, the sublime storyteller, calls us into the passion of telling our tale. But creating personal spiritual stories is an act of soul-making that does not happen automatically. It comes only as we risk stepping into the chaos of our lives and naming the angels that inhabit the shadows. It comes as we give expression to our struggle for individual meaning, identity, and truth, as we wrestle with angels, both light and dark, and celebrate the places where God stirs. In the crucible of story we become artists of meaning. There we meet God most surely.

∾

IT IS LATE CHRISTMAS EVE. The fire has burned to embers, the children are asleep. My husband is assembling a doll stroller. I hand him a screwdriver and as I lean back on the carpet my eyes light on a tiny blue and silver rocking horse on the Christmas tree. The ornament is a remnant of my childhood. As I stare at it, memories wander out of the past . . .

> *I am a child and it is nearly Christmas. I stand on a kitchen chair pummeling cookie dough with a rolling pin. I wallop the bag of flour right off the counter and*

it explodes in a cloud of white dust. I do not move, waiting for my mother's reaction. "What's your favorite cookie shape?" she asks. I find my voice. "A star." Smiling, she hands me the tin cutter. "Make lots of stars while I clean up," she says . . .

. . . My daddy lifts me off the seat of his truck and carries me deep into the cold woods to find a Christmas tree. I tramp by a dozen or more that he points out. On and on. Finally, I choose one. He says, "Yes, ma'am, I believe this one was worth waiting for." He chops it down, loads it onto his big shoulders, and holds my hand all the way back to the truck. . . .

Back home, I gaze at the freshly decorated tree . . . at a blue and silver rocking horse near the top. Mother calls me to the window and points out a star. It is unusually big and Bethlehem-bright. We lean on the sill and remember the holy night in a silence that is deeper and richer than words.

The door in time closes as quietly as it opened. I stare at the ornament, thinking how precious memories are. They live in our hearts and minds, waiting to whisper back to us. Sometimes they come in difficult times, giving strength and hope. Or they come simply to touch us with affection.

It occurs to me that perhaps the memories most likely to resonate do not fall happenstance into our lives. They are created. A pan of cookie stars in a warm kitchen. Holding hands in the woods.

Sandy has finished the doll stroller; a new doll is tucked inside. Silence, now. Then the rustle of a small nightgown at the door. "Mama!" cries Ann, spying the stroller. She hugs the doll. I blink at her. Now what? She has spoiled the surprise.

"Want to carry your new doll to bed?" I ask.

She nods. They will wake up on Christmas morning already friends. Maybe as important, perhaps on a Christmas Eve yet to come, she, too, will remember.

❧

ON A HOT AND HAZY SUMMER DAY, under the canopy of an oak tree, my son Bob and his buddy Michael, both nine, are swinging on the ropes that dangle from the tree limbs.

They've spent part of the afternoon watching the Lone Ranger and Tonto on television. Now they ride the old rope swings . . . a cowboy and an Indian brave, shouting, "Hi-ho, Silver, away!" It's all wonderful magic that rolls like a tumbleweed out of their imagination.

But as I watch from the kitchen window, the magic is broken. Michael slips from the swing and lands on a tree root. He picks himself up, staring at his palm and a slight trickle of blood winding onto his wrist. I shake my head at all the cuts and scratches of summer. Already that morning Bob had cut his thumb on a tin can buried in the alley, and I had treated and bandaged the wound.

I reach for the trusty box of Band-Aids and make my way outside. But as I approach the oak, I notice the two of them locked together in whispers. My son peels off his bandage and lifts his tin-can cut toward Michael. Then in a secret moment under the tree, the magic that had been interrupted suddenly resumes. The two boys touch their wounds together just as Tonto and the Lone Ranger had done . . . solemnly becoming "blood brothers." And when they are finished, the pain in Michael's face has vanished.

I treat the wound and slip away, sure that something special has happened across the landscape of this ordinary summer day.

∽

MY SEVEN-YEAR-OLD DAUGHTER sat in my grandmother's lap, moving her finger along the folds of Grandma's face.

"Those are my wrinkles," her great-grandmother said. "They mean I'm getting old."

Later, Ann asked me if wrinkles hurt and I pulled Margery Williams' classic, *The Velveteen Rabbit*, from the shelf and read it to her.

It's the story of a new toy rabbit that came to live in a little boy's nursery. More than anything, the rabbit yearned to the know the secret of becoming "real." One day he asked Skin Horse, who was so old his brown coat was rubbing off, how to become real. "Real isn't how you're made," he told the rabbit. "It's a thing that happens to you. When a child loves you for a long, long time . . . then you become Real." The rabbit then asked, "Does it hurt?"

"Sometimes," he answered. "Generally by the time you

are Real, most of your hair has been loved off, and your eyes drop out and you get loose in the joints and very shabby. But these things don't matter at all because once you are Real, you can't be ugly, except to people who don't understand."

"You see, Ann, Grandma is just getting 'real.' That's all."

Ann bounded off, but I was left to consider for the first time that growing old could be a wondrous passage. The markings of it didn't matter, except to those who didn't understand. What mattered was becoming "real." What mattered was loving and being loved for a long, long time.

~

THIS IS A PECULIAR STORY I'm about to tell you. Yet, it is true.

My father-in-law died on September tenth, a sudden death at the age of sixty.

Devastated, my mother-in-law carried her grief through the autumn and then winter, through all those barren, dead weeks. As spring came and woke the world, her pain was still locked within her. The jonquils pushed up like breaths of life from beneath the earth, and the lone dogwood tree in her front yard burst into new life, opening its delicate pink buds.

Mom watched the tree from the window—it had always been her favorite tree, as well as my father-in-law's—but she could not find much comfort.

Summer withered away, children walked back to school and a leaf or two drifted off the trees in her yard.

On September tenth Mom's grief grew intense. As she wandered to the mailbox, however, her eyes lit on the dogwood tree. In the center of the browning yard, under a golden, almost autumn sun, the tree had burst into bloom. It was covered in new pink blossoms. Spring blossoms on the doorstep of autumn. This began Mom's journey out of grief.

Later that day as I stared at the oddly flowering tree, at the petals that had come back on that day, of all days, I felt awed by mystery. By the myriad ways God comforts.

〜

A GROUP OF US WERE IN A "storytelling" session in which people gathered in circles to tell stories from their lives. One of the participants had attended a "clowning" workshop just before the session and showed up wearing a white clown face and a gigantic red smile painted ear to ear. When it came time for her to tell her story, I expected a happy tale to match her face. Instead she told about her husband's death seven years earlier and how she had been stuck in grief ever since.

It was such a contradiction to see her tell this story of pain while wearing a big red clown smile, and I mentioned the irony of it.

She thought a moment. "You know, maybe that's why I've been trapped in grief. For seven years I've been crying on the inside and smiling on the outside. Creating the illusion of happiness was easier than facing the hurt."

When I ache inside with a problem, I sometimes think of that woman as a reminder that help and healing do not come when we pretend and mask our pain, but rather when we are honest and admit our need.

∾

I REMEMBER A STORY my grandmother used to tell when I was a child.

A ragged little girl stood on tiptoe at a store window. It

was full of Christmas magic—a gleaming red tricycle, a doll with golden curls, a fuzzy panda bear. Her eyes widened with wonder.

Just then a friend happened by. "Too bad you won't be getting anything for Christmas," she said.

"Oh, but I will!" said the ragged child.

"But you said yourself your parents are broke and there would be no presents."

The girl pressed her face against the window. "That's true. But I asked God to send me something."

The friend shook her head and skipped off.

After Christmas the two girls met again. "Did you get your present?" asked the skeptical friend.

The little girl dropped her head. "No."

"God didn't answer your prayer," her friend said.

"I'm sure God told someone to bring me a gift," the ragged child said. "But I guess they forgot."

IN *ALICE IN WONDERLAND* the White Queen practiced believing six impossible things every morning before breakfast.

My daughter Ann and I became intrigued. "Maybe we should try it," I said.

Next morning when I woke her for school, we conjured up six "impossible" things to believe in. "I believe I will make a hundred on my science test today," Ann said. Since that was her hardest subject, I knew this was a leap of faith.

My turn. "I believe I can write two speeches before tomorrow," I muttered. Foolishly, I'd agreed to fill in at the last minute for a conference speaker who'd canceled. It seemed like an impossible feat.

That afternoon Ann bounded in the house from school. "What did you make on your science test?" I asked.

"A hundred!" she cried.

I looked down at two finished speeches on my desk. How limited the world would be if we confined ourselves and God to what we think is impossible.

LAST SPRING I SAT under a funeral awning in an Albany, Georgia, cemetery while my grandmother was buried. I watched a dragonfly cut persistent zagging lines in the air above the coffin as if performing some cryptic eulogy, and wondered at the significance of her dying on the first day of spring.

On the day the world was waking up to new life, she had closed her eyes and died. It was a kind of irony, and I sat there trying to scrutinize the small coincidence, wondering whether there were some meaning to it. But, as often happens in moments like that, all scrutiny failed and I was left with nothing but a memory. An odd memory, too, on the occasion of a funeral.

It is the day before Easter and I am eight years old. My mother has made me a lavender parasol to match my Easter dress. Before it was recycled, the parasol was an old umbrella, battered by one too many rainstorms. Mother stripped it down to its skeleton and refashioned it in organdy and lace. Now it is a purple spectacle, as impractical as hyacinths.

When I model it for my grandmother on Easter Eve, I know how peacocks feel. I walk differently under its small dome of violet light, feeling like I am newly arrived on the planet.

My grandmother smiles. "Why don't you twirl it a little while you walk?" she says. I am impressed with her suggestion and practice spinning it as I glide down the living room runway. It is not a walk so much as a strut, a walk so full of glorious feeling that I am in danger of levitating.

"I don't know about twirling it," Mother says, seeing how dazzled I am becoming by my own splendor.

"Oh, for heaven's sake, let her spin the parasol," Grandmother tells her.

"Well, all right," Mother says, looking at me, "but I don't want you opening it up inside the church."

This seems to me like the waste of a good opportunity, and seeing how my face falls, Grandmother doesn't see why I couldn't open it for a little while during Sunday school, especially if I was sitting by the window and the sun was coming in hot on my back.

On Easter morning I sit through the Sunday school lesson with my parasol open wide like I am the maharajah of Easter. I do this knowing my grandmother would secretly approve.

At the graveside, the minister was offering a lovely tribute, but I was lost in my own thoughts. The picture of my grandmother I love best was taken at my mother's wedding. She wore a saucy hat cocked wildly on one side of her head. Mother once pulled it out of the cedar chest and showed it to me. I was not prepared for the shocking array of pink, rose, and lavender chiffon, the kind of hat that causes people to nudge one another in the ribs. *It was her lavender parasol*, I think.

I remembered that in 1930, after she had acquired a red convertible Auburn touring car, she took her three children —while my grandfather stayed home to work—and struck off on a spirited adventure across the country, all the way to California. I imagined her doing it because she woke up one morning with the desire to seize life all over again. My grandmother carried inside her a certain renewing flame that is hard to define.

Perhaps it is best described as the impertinent, parasol-spinning spirit that generally flares up in the human soul in the spring of the year, wanting to make life new and alive again.

Not long ago my mother had showed me a piece of paper she had found beside my grandmother's bed the day she died. It said, "May I wake ready for that daily, yet greatest of gifts—a fresh start."

As the graveside service ended that day in South Georgia, I was still wondering about the coincidence of Sue Yarborough, ninety-eight years old, dying on the first day of spring. I do not know whether there is meaning in such things. Maybe it was some subtle object lesson of how endings and beginnings interact, I cannot really say. I only felt the rightness of her timing.

I wandered by her casket, lingering a minute in the rich tenderness of good-byes. I was thinking that I would love to give my lavender parasol one more twirl. I was thinking that I would like to strap on life all over again and wear it like a saucy hat until I died.

∾

I BELIEVE IN STORIES. The world has enough dogma. It's stories we need more of, stories that reverence the still, small voice that sings our life. As Anthony de Mello observed,

"The shortest distance between a human being and Truth is a story." Jesus, himself, told stories about the most common things in the world: a lost sheep, a seed that falls on rocky ground, a woman who sweeps her house in search of a coin, a man whose son runs away from home.

All personal theology should begin with the words: *Let me tell you a story*.

AWARENESS

I THINK OF ATTENTIVENESS as the capacity to be one-pointed, listening at ever-deepening levels of awareness. Ultimately our ability to do this is derived from the meditative practices and contemplative exercises that we undertake. They help us awaken and fine-tune our attention.

It goes like this. Find a practice and do it with discipline. Then bring the quality of that attentiveness to your external experience. We could call this practical mysticism.

Because in the beginning I forgot to remember, I used reminders. When the clock bonged on the hour in my house, it was an invitation to be attentive. Every time I climbed stairs, for some reason it was a cue to be attentive. In such ways awareness spreads out.

This exquisite quality of engaging in sustained, nondiscursive, active awareness becomes an *intentionality* that penetrates other aspects of life.

The idea is that in the flow of daily experience we situate ourselves deeply in our interior place. We let the inner dialogue and flow of images that suffuse our ordinary consciousness cease, or at least let them pass, and find ourselves aware and focused.

I can get very disengaged from life that's happening right now. My worst case scenario was the afternoon I got in my car to run an errand. Ten minutes later I found myself in front of my daughter's school, where I drove five days a week to pick her up. The problem was that this was a Saturday and I had been on my way to the dry cleaners. Lost in an automatic mental flow with a life of its own, I was grossly inattentive to the here and now.

Someone pointed out to me that the words *now, here,* and *nowhere* have the same arrangement of letters, but differ when a small space is inserted. Likewise a fine space separates us from experiencing our life as nowhere or now here.

Attentiveness is entering fully the moment you are currently in, no matter how hassling and mundane, and simply being present with it.

～

AT NINE THIRTY ON AN AUGUST NIGHT filled with lightning bugs and cricket sounds, my children and I lie in the backyard waiting for the Perseid meteor shower. The sky stretches over us like a dark, deserted stage. There is no trace of a shooting star. The grass begins to itch. The troops grow restless.

Then it happens—so quickly I catch my breath. One, two, three golden balls of fire streak across the darkness. "Oh, look . . . look!" I cry.

"Wow-w-w-w," says my son, his voice trailing after them.

One after another they come, blazing across the heavens. And without warning, a spell of reverence falls across the backyard. We lie in silence while the ground beneath us grows holy and God's presence burns across the sky, yet deep and luminous inside me too. It is a rare moment. Not because the sight is so spectacular, but because I am aware of it. Because I have been taken out of myself. My children and I have stepped out of our familiar world into wonder and beauty, and have discovered the Creator in the midst of it.

❧

ONE SUMMER DAY in my adolescence, I went to the lake with a friend and stood at the water's edge, gazing at the sunlight bobbing on the surface. Ribbons of blue water curled between my toes. Behind me, tall grass rippled. Above, clouds floated in silence. The world seemed like an incandescent invitation.

"Come on," I called to Evelyn. "Let's swim."

"The water looks murky," she replied. "And I would hate to risk my sinuses flaring up again."

I went without her. I plunged into the cool waters, then burst up into hot, dazzling light. As I did, I saw Evelyn huddled on her scrap of towel, not really seeing or feeling the world. If there is actually a defining moment when we decide whether to take on the full hazard of life or play it safe, this was likely mine.

Jesus spoke of abundant living. He said, "I am come that they might have life, and that they might have it more abundantly." Maybe, in part, he was saying that he came to wake us to the joys of existence, to coax us off our towels.

∾

Sir Christopher Wren designed St. Paul's Cathedral in London, a towering and magnificent work of carvings, columns, arches, and spires that took thirty-five years to build. He is buried in the cathedral, beneath a plain and simple slab. Barely noticeable and void of trappings, his tomb bears only this inscription: "If you seek his monument, look around you."

In the end, the only monument that matters may be the work of love we carve into the lives around us.

∾

One bright, frozen day in downtown Atlanta, I stood outside a soup kitchen as a line of homeless and hungry people gathered. My husband and I had come to help serve the noon meal. As I neared the door, I noticed a woman wearing a thin coat, a ski cap, and *one* glove. She clasped her cold, unprotected hand in her gloved hand, trying to rub some warmth into it.

"I see you lost a glove," I said to her.

"No," she replied, smiling. "I *found* a glove."

❧

THE LANGUAGE OF GOD is life itself, and I live with the unquenchable need to take my life in my hands and try to read the divine alphabet written upon it.

❧

RECENTLY ON THE EVE of my birthday a woman said to me with a completely serious face, "When I turn fifty, I want to become *notorious*."

"Notorious for what?" I asked.

This seemed to throw her. "Well, I'm not sure," she said. "I haven't gotten that far along with the idea."

Becoming notorious for the sake of becoming notorious was a peculiar idea to me. Besides that, had she consulted a dictionary for the meaning of notorious? I went home and looked it up. It said: "Notorious—widely but infamously known or talked about."

I couldn't see the appeal. But after my conversation with the woman, practically against my will, I began to entertain a thought: *What would I want to be notorious for at fifty?*

I was still secretly working on it when a group of women gathered to help me celebrate my birthday. For our evening's entertainment I brought out my book of Mary Oliver's poems and suggested we take turns reading. As bemused glances were exchanged, it occurred to me if I did ever become notorious, it would not be for bacchanalian parties.

I read last, choosing a poem with the cheery title "When Death Comes." I read along unsuspecting till I got to a line in which Oliver writes about coming to the end and wanting to say that she has spent her life married to amazement.

Suddenly something unexpected happened to me. My throat tightened. My eyes filled. I don't mean sad tears, but the kind that leak from something brimming.

I looked at the faces around the room. They seemed beautiful and shining to me. I glanced at a common white lily in a vase and honestly, the sight nearly wiped me out. It was *that* impertinently gorgeous. Out of nowhere, plain and simple objects were rising up to show off their flame. The divine, unnameable spark. I couldn't think what to name the feeling except amazement at life. It was as if something fell from my eyes and I saw everything just as it is.

One second I was going along in a jaded marriage with life (because let's face it, the intimacy can fade after a while if you don't work on the relationship) when it rode in and swept me off my feet. I learned to be in love with life again. And I didn't even know the romance had slipped.

"Life is a spell so exquisite that everything conspires to break it," wrote Emily Dickinson. Somehow I'd begun moving through life on automatic pilot, half-seeing, half-here, abducted by the dreaded small stuff. But the evening of my party, I realized all over again: We will have a true and blissful marriage to life only to the extent we are *aware*.

So. That's how I resolved the question about what I wished to become notorious for at fifty. Let it be for nothing more than harboring a wild amazement at life. Let it be for choking up at poetry and the sight of human faces. For falling into easy rapture over lilies and all the other run-of-the-mill marvels that make up life. Let me become notorious for going around with my bridal veil tossed back and my mouth saying I do. Renewing my vows with life. Every day. A hundred times a day.

∞

AT TWENTY-NINE, spiritually hungry and intensely restless, I read a book that changed my life: *The Seven Storey Mountain*. It is Thomas Merton's autobiographical account of growing up and entering a Trappist monastery. At the time, I knew absolutely nothing about monasteries, much less the contemplative life. I had grown up in a Baptist family in a small town in Georgia. My religious education had taught me that the kingdom of God is within, but somehow I had never grasped the meaning or immensity of this until I read Merton's book. His words woke me to the intoxicating reality of the interior life, igniting a dormant longing in my own soul to experience God. I found out for myself what the mystical poet Rumi meant when he wrote that his soul is a "furnace happy with fire."

As I entered my thirties, I found myself yearning for ways to commune with the deep unquenchable mystery I'd stumbled upon. In other words, I wanted to learn how to care for my soul. I devoured classic contemplative literature and went on monastic retreats, some of them to Merton's own monastery, but my forays into solitude and meditative moments were difficult and infrequent. The truth is that I spent far more time wishing for contemplative experiences than actually having them.

It was excruciatingly easy to lose touch with the inner life of the soul. There was such a profusion of demand and complexity, so many to-do lists, the unceasing compulsion to accomplish something. When I read that the Chinese pictograph for busyness is "heart killing," I felt the truth of that in my bones.

In the midst of this struggle to care for my soul, I read Wordsworth's poem, "The Prelude," in which he writes about "spots of time" that nourish and repair the soul. I believe he was referring to brief, concentrated moments—little epiphanies—that inflame us with a sense of the holy.

I began to search for spots of time here and there in my day. I found them by stopping. Just stopping. Some of my favorite words that Jesus spoke are, "Come away by yourself to a lonely place and rest a while." I began to "come away" to a nook somewhere in the house or the yard where I would spend five minutes or less sitting still and receding into the quiet core of myself.

Putting the soul at rest in this way is more than merely restorative, it is how many Christian mystics describe contemplative prayer. One is simply finding one's being in God.

Caring for my soul turned out to be simply that—spots of time in which to be.

AVAILABILITY

O N A BITTER NIGHT in January, I sit on a train that rumbles away from the airport in Atlanta. I stare at the blackness beyond the window, but mostly what I see is my own reflection lit brightly on the pane. Tired and morose, I look away. I'm supposed to be flying home to South Carolina, but minutes before my departure, the entire airport closed because of an impending ice storm. "Nothing's flying out of here tonight, lady," the man at the boarding gate said. I didn't relish the idea of spending the night in a plastic chair, so I called my brother-in-law in the Atlanta suburbs and begged for shelter. He told me to take the train to a station near his house, that he would try to make it through the ice to pick me up. Try, he said. I sigh so audibly people turn to stare.

It's a long ride. At each stop a few more people get off and vanish into the storm. Soon there are only three of us. A middle-aged woman sits across from me. I look at her for the first time and notice that she's crying. As she wipes tears with the back of her hand, her gaze lingers on my face. A look full of ache and searching. She's asking for my attention. She wants me to fling open my heart and take her in.

I feel sad for her, but what can I do? She's carrying her own troubles and I can't fix them. My inhibitions rise sharply, then blend into tiredness, anxieties about the storm, disappointment at not getting home. I look away from her, retreating into the murmur of the train. Quietly, uncomfortably unavailable.

For the next two days I sit ensconced in my brother-in-law's den watching snow and ice build a crystal fortress outside the window. I think entirely too much about the woman on the train. She's like a song on the radio that gets stuck in your head.

The second night she comes powerfully into my dreams. She sits across from me, this time in a rowboat. Her tears gush over the tiny precipice of her eyelids like waterfalls. The boat is filling up with this sad water, and I realize that if I don't do something, we're going to sink. *Both* of us. I try bailing the tears, but that gets us nowhere. She keeps crying. Finally I stop and stare into those irrepressible eyes. When I do, the tears start to dry up, but if I look away they start again.

The dream cracks my heart, and I wake with solemn wonder, reunited with an old truth: People with profound human needs and suffering do not, as I have half-imagined and half-wished, travel in a boat separate from mine. In ways I have scarcely appreciated, we are all in the same boat, and I can't be unavailable to their suffering without jeopardizing my own soul. We will sink together or we will float together.

In the worst way I want to live the train ride over. The divine wisdom in the dream pointed out that it wasn't necessary for me to try and fix the woman's pain, but simply to be available and present with my heart. What was required was that I peer into her eyes, the ancient windows of the soul, and truly see her. What was needed was that I unwaveringly take her in.

The Georgia ice melts and I return home, but something about the episode has become a burr along the skin of my soul. One morning as I read, I come upon the words of the great Christian mystic, Mechtild of Magdeburg:

"How should one live?
Live
Welcoming
to all."

I try to explicate the words. Make them transcendent, pastel, a sweet, distant thing for saints and mystics. But every time they drag me back to the woman on the train—this woman who has somehow become the archetype of the stranger, the suffering other. Live, welcoming all. I'm forced to ponder the meaning of really living my life this way.

I begin to observe myself in the presence of others, friends and strangers alike, and I'm surprised by the level of my availability. I watch my restless heart, the mercurial way my mind sweeps from one thing to another, the way my ego holds forth, keeping me abreast of my own expectations, wants, and preoccupations, criticizing, comparing, competing, imposing views. I realize that I can be with someone, but on a deeper level I'm not available to them at all. I have attention deficit disorder of the soul.

I decide to take up availability as a discipline, as a form of spiritual practice, like meditation, prayer, or Scripture read-ing. What if I practice receiving each person with the whole of my heart, or what might be called mindful availability?

What would it mean to be utterly available to the one before me? There's a Zen adage that points to the impor-tance of an undivided consciousness: When you eat, just eat. When you sit, just sit. Mindful availability would say: When you sit with a crying woman on a train, just sit with her. Do it with all your mind and heart and soul. Be fully present to her without this other agenda going on at the sidelines. In other words, do it without passing judgment on her, wanting to convert her to your point of view, desir-ing her appreciation, wondering what others on the train might think, worrying about the weather, or generally get-ting caught up in one's own feelings, desires, and opinions of the moment. Do it the way Mary sat at the feet of Jesus— with an undivided heart.

Such deep availability requires a hospitality that receives people as they are, without necessarily seeking to cure, fix, or repair their problems. When you practice mindful availabil-ity, you are simply there with your heart flung open.

THROUGHOUT THE WINTER as I struggle to practice mindful availability, I keep stumbling over something unavoidable. The opposite of availability is not unavailability, but an overcrowded heart.

In February, my husband and I attend a party where a lot of strangers stand around holding tiny plates of food, trying to make conversation. Midway through it, I realize that my interaction with these people has been more like a silent collision of egos than anything else. I've been full of myself, back again riding a train where my own image lights up every window. I've overflowed with my own ideas, with a variety of self-motivated feelings, and I see clearly how my fullness undermines my ability to be present, how it erodes the possibility of mindful availability.

A friendly, empty space must be created *within* the host. I think of the bowl in my study, the one I made myself from a small, round gourd. I spent a whole day cleaning out the inside, painting it green, waxing it to a sheen. I thought I'd fill it with something. But I never did. Now I see that I was engaged in creating a vessel of emptiness, a thing to hold a beautiful nothing.

In March I see the movie *Dead Man Walking*, not anticipating the way it's about to plunge me into another confrontation with my heart. I watch as Catholic Sister Helen Prejean (played by Susan Sarandon) visits Matthew Poncelet, who's on death row for kidnapping, rape, and murder. She has made herself available to him in the most mindful and loving way, and I'm wondering if I could do what this sister is doing. She tells him, "You are a son of God, Matthew Poncelet." Visibly touched, he begins to cry, "Nobody ever called me a son of God before. Called me a 'son-of-a-you-know-what' lots of times, but never no son of God. Thank you for loving me."

The sister also visits the parents of the young woman who was murdered. Sitting in their kitchen, she tells them she's come because she wants to be available to them, to help them, to pray with them. They assume her visit means she's no longer involved with Poncelet, and she's forced to explain that, to the contrary, she's agreed to be his spiritual advisor.

The parents react with shock. "How can you come here?" the girl's mother says.

"Sister, I think you need to leave this house right now!" the father tells her. "You can't have it both ways. You can't befriend that murderer and expect to be our friend too!"

After the movie, the mother's question remains hauntingly clear in my mind: "How can you come here?" Yes, I'd like to know the answer to that too. I want to know what sort of spirituality compels someone to be available to both the family of a murdered girl and the murderer. I marvel at the audacity of it.

I am compelled to uncover my own hidden and unconscious notions about whom I will open my heart to and to whom I prefer to keep it shuttered. I discover that while I'm making progress emptying myself and making my availability more mindful, I have a whole secret ledger of restrictions concerning who's deserving of it. There are some folks, I realize, so ideologically and politically different from me I have no real intention of being available to them.

"Welcome *all*," Mechtild wrote. *All.*

Jesus, who was perhaps the most accomplished practitioner of unrestricted availability the world has seen, told us, "If anyone strikes you on the right cheek, turn the other also;

and if anyone wants to sue you and take your coat, give your cloak as well." Be available to all, he's saying. Welcome them on their own terms and not your own. If I take Jesus seriously, I will have to practice mindful availability with the group that slaps my cheek with their opposing political and religious ideas.

This seems a quantum leap for my human heart—to be mindfully available no matter how offensive the person. No matter how many light years apart we are ideologically. I think of all the Americans of different races, genders, religions, politics, sexual orientations, and philosophies who are slugging it out in culture wars that increasingly polarize us. I wonder what will break the impasse, how we will ever transcend our differences, and it occurs to me that unrestricted availability offers a beginning.

In California where I'm to speak at a religious conference, I discover how good life is at giving us opportunities to practice what we profess. After my final talk—a supportive presentation on women's spirituality—an obviously angry man leaps from his chair and charges straight toward me.

"Women like you make me sick!" he says. "You go

around questioning things that shouldn't be tampered with."
Anger rises in me, but frankly I'm too stunned to speak. As
he goes on in more detail, I want to give him a piece of my
mind, to defend myself, to lay him low. But even as these
inclinations mount, I remember the practice of unrestricted
availability I've committed myself to.

With all the strength of will I can muster, I take a
moment to breathe, to step back and become as empty as I
can. Suddenly it's as if I'm observing the whole wrathful
scene from a perspective other than my wounded and embat-
tled ego. I realize the man is reacting out of fear. He's made
me a target because my ideas are threatening the secure way
he's constructed his religious world.

The brimstone I want to rain down on him goes mysteriously cold. I won't go so far as to say I have sweet, warm
feelings toward the man. But that doesn't matter. Sweet,
warm feelings have little to do with mindful and unrestricted availability. What matters is the intention of the
heart, and this intention enables me to do for him what I
didn't do for the woman on the train. I invite him aside to a
quiet place where we sit down together. "I'll listen to what-

ever you want to tell me," I say. I gaze into his eyes, offering him the unwavering attention of my heart, as best I can. Somehow I carve out a small, egoless space inside and welcome him.

Gradually the fight goes out of him. "You know," he says, "I realize there are some things more important than the differences between us. I'm sorry."

I don't ask him what that "more important" thing is, but I think I can tell by his face. That something is love.

When I deplore the rigors and demands of a mindful and unrestricted availability, I think again how we travel the universe upon this tiny planet, knee-deep in the sorrows of its inhabitants. And like the dream says: You can bail tears all you want, but the saving thing has more to do with the hospitality of your heart. Together we sink. Together we float. Together. That's the small, tender mercy of the ride.

∽

AS NIGHT SETTLED upon the sprawling hospital, I prepared to make nursing rounds on the ninth floor pediatric wing.

Tiptoeing into a darkened ward, I beamed my flashlight on the sleeping children. A tiny kittenlike whimper drifted from the corner bed. I turned my pool of light on Amy. Her brown eyes spilled over with tears. Tomorrow Amy would lose her tonsils.

"What's the matter?" I asked, wrapping my arm around her.

"It's dark and I'm all by myself," she said.

"Then why don't I stay with you?" I said.

Though she tried hard to be brave, my presence could not stop her crying. Finally, fearing she would get no rest, I gave her a sedative. But even the medicine was useless. Her tears grew into sobs.

In desperation I phoned her father at home. Soon he stood by Amy's bed. She slipped her hand into his, closed her eyes and slept.

When I have stumbled into dark places in life and felt alone, I have discovered a presence that has calmed my mind, relaxed my body, and anchored my soul. I find peace that I cannot find elsewhere when I sit with this holiness.

∽

WE WERE TWO STRANGERS on a ferry. We leaned on the rail, side by side, watching the African landscape fade into the river. I eyed her with a sideways glance. She was Kenyan. I was American. She had beautiful black skin and her head was coiled with bright *kitange* cloth. I, white-skinned, wore blue jeans. She had bare feet. I had on tennis shoes. Our eyes met briefly, then we looked away as we shrank deeper into our own separate and distant worlds. The only thing we seemed to have in common was our wariness of each other.

The boat lurched. A wave popped against the side, dousing us with water. We looked at each other in surprise, mouths open, faces sopping wet, both of us dripping, and suddenly we burst out laughing. She unwound her headdress and dabbed first at my face, then her own. We smiled at each other, pointing to our wet clothes and chattered our way across the river with smatterings of Swahili and English. Like magic, we became friends, drawn together by the ribbons of laughter.

It must be true what Victor Borge said: "Laughter is the shortest distance between two people."

⌒

LATE ONE WINTER NIGHT it snows in South Carolina. When the sun comes up, a dazzling white quilt lays across our small backyard.

"Oh-h-h, Mommy." In the bedroom both children cling to the windowsill speechless. It is their first snow.

I bundle them up. At first they tread slowly into the strange white world. Crunch. Crunch. It is the sound of eggshells beneath their boots.

I shiver on the steps. "Watch me!" shouts Bob. He falls backward into the snow . . . a toppled snowman.

"Wow!" I exclaim.

"Watch me, Mama!" calls Ann. Now she falls backward in the snow. Her head pops up.

"Did you see?"

"I saw," I tell her. "That was beautiful."

"Watch this," yells Bob. He reaches for a limb of the crab apple tree. It bends down like a dump truck and empties its load on his head. From inside the flying flakes come a big gasp and a weak giggle. "Did you watch?" he shouts.

"You were great," I cry. "Just great."

My toes are getting numb. I turn for the door. But Ann calls to me from the top of the backyard hill. "Look . . . look at me!" She soars down on a flattened cardboard box, her South Carolina sled.

"You were fantastic," I shout. Her face beams.

Watch me. Watch me. It is a steady refrain. Finally I slip into the house, remembering the shine on their cold faces and the sure way they drew back their shoulders as I reassured them with grand superlatives. I am struck at how deep the need for approval and admiration is cut into their little souls. How easy, yet necessary it is to tell them how wonderful they are.

HE CAME CLUTCHING A HANDFUL of daisies. He came just as he did every day, passing the nurse's desk, where I worked, down the hospital corridor to his daughter's room. She was nearly six now, shut away in a world of unconsciousness and coma. Yet sometimes I heard him, as he sat by her bedside, talking to her about her dog or her brother or even the weather.

I entered the room that day as he was stroking her hair

and telling her a story. The daisies drooped over the sides of a little plastic cup, positioned where she would see them if she opened her eyes. He paused when he saw me and patted his daughter's hand. She was so still that for an instant I looked with relief at the rise and fall of the sheet over her chest.

I wondered how he sat here day after day, without ever getting a response. Without a thank-you for the flowers, without her eyes following his stories, without a smile, or a hug, or even the flutter of an eyelash. All he ever got in return was her slow, comatose breathing and the awful stillness.

"It must be hard to keep giving so much love when she's . . . like this," I said.

"I suppose," he answered. "But I'll keep coming and bringing the flowers and telling these stories even if she's oblivious to it, because I love her whether or not she loves me back."

I do not know of a more sublime love than that: unconditional, eternal, tender, unrelenting.

⟋

FROM THE WINDOW I NOTICE a small brown wren huddled on the grass beneath the bird feeder, struggling to fly. The frigid wind bends the branches of the crab apple tree. Fifteen minutes pass. He cannot seem to find the strength. Is he sick? Too young? Too weak? It seems sad. But I suppose there is little I can do for him.

Suddenly my attention is drawn to another wren that flies to the feeder. I am astonished as she begins to toss seed with her beak from the ledge of the feeder down to the grass below. The kernels fall upon the little bird and he pecks at them, satisfying his hunger. The next time I pass the window he's gone.

All day I watch the wrens at the feeder, thinking how we are put here not only to partake, but to feed the hungers of those around us. *Drop seed. Drop seed.*

MY HUSBAND AND I plodded up the steps of a shelter for the homeless as a gust of wind whisked the last bit of light from the sky. The resident manager ushered us into a large room lined with rows of cots. I couldn't help but notice a young man in a tattered green suit and canary-yellow tie moving from cot to cot, person to person, clutching a blue album. "Wanna see my book?" he asked, revealing a gap-toothed grin. No one wanted to look at it.

"That's James," the resident manager said. "He's one of a kind. A simpleminded fellow. Can't read or write. But he has a good heart."

After dinner Sandy and I wandered into the lobby. I noticed James in his sunny yellow tie, sitting by himself, absorbed in his scrapbook. I tried to slip by but James was motioning to me. "Wanna see my book?"

Reluctantly I joined him on an old vinyl sofa. He slid over so I did not have to sit on a gaping tear. I gazed at his eager, childlike expression, swallowed hard and opened the book he reverently handed me. Inside was a curious collection: a paper napkin from a fast-food restaurant, a bluebird's feather, a church bulletin, a faded birthday card, a pocket calendar . . .

James told me about each item—how he'd eaten the most delicious meal of his life in the restaurant, how he'd found the feather in Piedmont Park where he shared his afternoons with the birds. The church bulletin came from a mission where he'd been welcomed. The card was on his cot on his birthday. The calendar was last year's Christmas "gift" from a store clerk.

Some pages were inscribed with autographs. "They're all my friends," he said proudly. One signature was from a man who'd helped him find clothes, another from a lady who brought meals.

Gradually I understood. The album represented James's list of blessings. Blessings he read and reread.

He reached into the front pocket of his suit and pulled out a stubby pencil. "Would you sign my book?" he asked.

I felt the back of my throat tighten. "To my new friend," I wrote, then signed my name and read the words back to him. His gesture in response was so soft I almost missed it. He brushed a finger across my words, as if caressing the thought. Then he stood up, tucked his album of blessings under his arm and said good night.

∽

WHILE VISITING A LODGE in the mountains, my husband and I found a row of rocking chairs on the porch. We settled into a couple and started to rock. More guests joined us until soon six chairs were rocking.

Gradually the chairs fell into exactly the same rhythm.

"Look how our chairs are all moving together now," I said to a man on my right.

"If you hang several pendulums on a wall and give them enough time, they'll do the same thing," he told me. "Even insects that chirp or blink will eventually fall into unison. It's known as entrainment. It means that two or more rhythmic beings will gradually alter their movements until they are locked in sync."

I suspect the same mystery happens in the harmonizing of human hearts. Could we give ourselves such time?

∽

WHEN A SUFFERING IS SHARED, its weight is divided. And when a joy is shared, the delight is multiplied. We need each other.

COMPASSION

COMPASSION OFTEN ELUDES ME. I remember the time I wept before a television image of a homeless man lying in an American gutter. Three weeks later I stepped over a homeless man on a sidewalk in New York without looking back. As I strode away, I had the odd feeling that somewhere someone was looking at me, waiting for an explanation.

"Be compassionate as your Father is compassionate," Jesus said. Sometimes I wonder how seriously we have taken those words to heart. I only know there is too much suffering in the world. Too many homeless, hungry, abused, rejected, poor, lonely, sick, grieving, fragmented, defeated, lost, and oppressed. There are too many bombs, too many wars, too many squashed beetles. The world is hip-deep in tears. Compassion is not an option. It is a matter of survival.

∽

THE SUMMER I WAS TWELVE I went to a nursing home with a youth group. Frankly, I was there under duress. My mother had not heard my pleas that I be spared the unjust sentence of visiting a nursing home when my friends were enjoying the last day of summer vacation at the city swimming pool. Smarting from the inequity, I stood before this ancient-looking woman, holding a bouquet of crepe paper flowers. Everything about her saddened me—the worn-down face, the lopsided grin, the tendrils of gray hair protruding from a crocheted lavender cap. I thrust the bouquet at her. She looked at me, a look that pierced me to the marrow of my twelve-year-old bones. Then she spoke the words I haven't forgotten for all these years. "You didn't want to come, did you, child?"

The words stunned me. They were too painful, too powerful, too naked in their honesty. "Oh yes, I wanted to come," I protested.

A smile lifted one side of her mouth. "It's okay," she said. "You can't force the heart."

For a while I hated her for the rebuke. Then I passed it off as the harmless twittering of an old woman. Years later though, as I began to follow the labyrinth of my spiritual journey, I discovered the truth in her words.

You can't force the heart. Genuine compassion cannot be imposed from without. It doesn't happen simply by hearing a sermon on love, or being sent on a loving mission. How often have we set out to love the world—or even more difficult, to love some tiresome, undeserving, mule-headed person on our street—and given up, feeling exasperated, unappreciated, used, tired, burned out, or just plain cynical? The point is, you don't arbitrarily make up your mind to be compassionate so much as you choose to follow a journey that transforms your heart into a compassionate space.

Compassion, which is the very life of God within us, comes through a slow and often difficult metamorphosis deep within the human soul. It happens through a process. If we look closely at the workings of creation, we find that God nearly always works through process. Think of it. First there is a seed, then a sprout, then a blossom, and finally fruit. God does not begin with a butterfly, but with a larva that becomes a chrysalis and finally a creature with wings. Neither does God speak a star into existence, but sends dust floating into space, then interstellar gas that slowly heats up, and eons later a star is formed. Perhaps most mysterious of all is the unfolding process of ovum, fetus, baby, child, adolescent, adult. The universe is designed to move stage by stage, from incompletion to completion. Now why should we suppose that God has designed the heart any differently than the rest of creation?

It, too, has its stages.

We move from a false and separatist way of relating to the world, which I call being in the Collective They, to a union with our True Self, which means realizing the Authentic I, and finally to a sense of interconnectedness with all that is, which brings us to the birth of the Compassionate We.

∽

WHEN I WAS SIX YEARS OLD someone asked me, "What do you want to be when you grow up?" At that age, living in a small Georgia town in the 1950s, I could only think of four careers for women—they were the only stories I knew: teacher, nurse, secretary, and housewife. By some process of elimination, I picked nurse. From that moment on, I began to get little nurse kits for my birthdays. The librarian at school set aside the biography of Florence Nightingale for me. If someone cut their finger, I was called in as the designated bandager. At sixteen, my parents arranged for me to be a volunteer at the local hospital. Everyone expected me to be a nurse, and I was like wet cement taking on the expectations.

I got my Bachelor's degree in nursing and worked nine years—even taught nursing in a college—before I stopped and said to myself, "This is not who I am. I am not really a nurse inside. I'm a writer." By that time, the cement had hardened and I had some jackhammer work to do, breaking up the old identity imbedded within and releasing a new self. I had continued with nursing, not because it is a noble profession that stirred my deep gladness, but because I did not want to risk upsetting others'—not to mention my own—ingrained notion of who I was. I wanted to please. I wanted to protect myself from the uncertainty of starting over. In such ways our consciousness becomes centered in the outer roles and masks we wear, rather than in the True Self within.

I have had to struggle to pull myself from the Collective

They. At various times I have lived out of narrowly prescribed identities that I accepted and internalized from the Collective: dutiful and submissive wife, ever-sacrificing mother, armored career woman, perfectionist, pleaser, performer, good little girl who never colored outside the lines drawn for her. Sometimes I was so busy being tuned in to outside ideas, expectations, and demands, I failed to hear the unique music in my soul. I forfeited my ability to listen creatively to my deepest self, to my own God within. I was wearing the name "They."

When I wear this name I am limited in my ability to relate to others in a genuinely compassionate way. I am separated from them by the masks that keep me from being real with them. Stuck in the Collective They, I am more apt to relate out of my ego needs, from the subtleties of my false selves and from mandates and demands placed on me from others, rather than love born in my own heart.

One day driving down the street, I asked myself, "Sue Monk Kidd, who are you?" Right away the obvious answers came. "You are Bob and Ann's mother, Sandy's wife, Leah and Ridley's daughter, a writer, a member of Grace Episcopal Church." All nice things. Then I asked myself. "So, if all those roles were stripped away, *then* who would you be?" The question jolted me. It brought me to stand before the bare mystery of my own being. Was there something deeper at the very core of me that was purely and truly my "I"?

I came to believe that my true identity goes beyond the outer roles I play. It transcends the ego. I came to understand that there is an Authentic "I" within—an "I Am," or divine spark within the soul.

Here is where our real selfhood is rooted, in the divine spark or seed, in the image of God imprinted on the human soul. The True Self is not our creation, but God's. It is the self we are in our depths. It is our capacity for divinity and transcendence.

Unraveling external selves and coming home to our real identity is the true meaning of soul work. I remember a time in my life when I actually thought the term "soul work" referred to the evangelistic effort of winning souls. That hints at how little attention I had paid to the soul as the seedbed of the divine life. I eventually found that the soul is more than an immortal commodity to win and save. It is the repository of the inner divine, the truest part of us.

A few years ago, struggling with false selves, wearing masks as if life were a masquerade party, I began to feel the suffocation that happens when we cut ourselves off from the True Self. I went away to a retreat center nestled among live oaks in the low country of South Carolina. I went to try and remember who I really was. I walked in the front door, and there tacked on the wall was a picture of the pregnant Madonna and these words:

> *This image represents each person who is trying to birth the Real Self, the* Imago Dei *that is taking shape within. For that conception to move to its fullness, we all need time to be quiet, to be reflective, to be centered in our deep places.*

During that retreat, I walked beneath the trees alone with God, alone with my True Self, praying wordless prayers, touching the space of mystery, going to my center. That time produced the energy needed to shift my awareness to an Authentic I, which is the necessary prelude for real compassion.

The emergence of one's Authentic I awakens a fresh awareness that God is the life of us all and we are one in God together.

Living out the Compassionate We means blending our

tears with the world's in a way that heals and creates community. The word *compassion* literally means *com* (with) *passion* (suffering). Compassion is not, therefore, having a sentimental feeling of pity; it is sharing the pain. It means a "suffering with" that flows from the life of God in the soul, not from ego motivations.

When compassion wakes up in us, we find ourselves more willing to become vulnerable, to take the risk of entering the pain of others. We open our lives to them in a genuine willingness to be known. We tell them our own story of suffering as a way of offering healing and hope. We feel their heart bleeding into ours; we catch their tears. We relieve their pain as much as we are able, and by relieving theirs, we relieve God's.

While reading Elie Weisel's book, *Night*, which is the chronicle of his suffering in a Nazi concentration camp, I came upon a story that spread before me a metaphoric picture of what it means to live in the Compassionate We as a community.

Nazi soldiers herded the Jews out of their barracks before dawn into thickly falling snow in order to wait for a train that would transport them to another camp. Having been without food and drink for three days, the Jews stood in the snow till evening, forbidden to sit or even bend over. The snow formed a layer on their shoulders. One thirsty man took out his spoon and began to eat the snow that had accumulated on the shoulders of the person in front of him. The act spread through the line until that collection of separate individuals, each of whom had been struggling alone with their pain, became a community sharing their suffering together.

The image burned into my mind, and I knew that in some way this is how we would survive as a human family, by becoming a place of nourishment for our brothers and sisters, by quietly shouldering their pain and their healing. We would survive as we became a We Community, sharing our sufferings in a great and holy act of compassion.

WHEN WE SEEK COMPASSION, we must remember that ultimately the heart cannot be forced. But it *can* become a womb where compassion is gestated and birthed. There we birth God. There we birth the name We. And with this holy name we will look with the eyes of the heart at all creatures, great and small, and walk gently upon God's bruised planet.

❧

SHE CAME UNINVITED to the sand dune. She was old and used a cane. I had seen her before, meandering along the beach in her outrageous straw hat, striking up long, uninvited conversations. Like the predictable sweep of a clock's hand, she would wander up to anyone, corralling them into a chat. Now here she was, on my sand dune.

"It's too pretty a day to work," she said, nodding at my notebook.

"I suppose," I replied, trying not to be drawn in.

She leaned on her cane and began to chatter away . . . about her late husband, about the grandchildren she rarely saw. I listened with a polite kind of patience, glancing once at my watch. Finally she took her leave and headed down the beach.

As I watched her go, I knew that she was a lonely woman who had only wanted to share a friendly moment. I felt my heart break a little at the loneliness in the world. Looking at her recede into the haze, I made myself a promise. I would climb the sand dune tomorrow. And wait.

~

THE DOCTOR'S FACE HINTED that the news was grim the moment he walked into Mr. Kelsy's room. "I'm sorry. You have cancer," he said. "We really should operate right away."

When the doctor left, Mr. Kelsy stared at the window in silence. I noticed he was trembling. I was a young nurse, inexperienced with suffering. I wanted to comfort him, but no words came. Absently I placed my hand on his shoulder, while rummaging in my mind for the right words.

He smiled at me. "Thank you," he said.

Thank you? For what? I stared at my hand on his shoulder. Could one small gesture communicate so much?

I have since learned never to underestimate the remarkable power of touch.

~

SHE HAD A PILE of freshly mended clothes on the front seat of her car. I noticed that a few buttons had been sewed back on with mismatched threads and the hems repaired with uneven stitches. "Who on earth did the repair work on these clothes?" I asked.

"My neighbor," she answered. "She's eighty years old and lives alone."

"But you're a fantastic seamstress. You could do a much better job than this," I said.

"Oh, probably so. But my neighbor needs to be needed far more than these clothes need to be perfect."

HE STANDS ON THE SIDEWALK beside the front door of the department store like an old cigar-store Indian, a tall, motionless man wearing no expression on his face, only sunglasses. He clutches a cigar box, which he thrusts out in a gesture of greeting and hope when footsteps come his way. The box rattles, the feet hurry by, and his arm sinks back against his seemingly wooden body.

As my seven-year-old daughter and I approach the door, I notice her steps slowing. She has caught sight of him. I've seen him on the streets before. But this is her first encounter with a beggar. She seems transfixed by the sight.

"What's he doing?" she asks too loudly.

"He's asking for money," I whisper.

Then comes the eternal question. "Why?"

"Because he's poor and he needs help," I say, hoping that satisfies her.

As we draw beside him, the cigar box is thrust in our direction. Ann stops and peeps inside it I grab her hand and pull her through the door.

As I'm browsing in the store, Ann wanders off. I find her at the front door where she's peering through the glass at the beggar.

"Mama, can we give him some money?" she asks.

"Well . . . sure we can." I snap open my purse. She peeps inside it just as she did with the cigar box. All I have is a dollar bill and two quarters.

I hand her the quarters. She stares at the two coins for a moment as if there is something important going on inside her. She says, "Mama, give him the dollar, too, and I'll pay you back from my allowance."

Her words cut through all my distraction and unconcern, and touch me deeply. I hand her the dollar. I watch her walk shyly over to the beggar and gaze into his blind face a long moment before she lays the money in his box.

It's one of those moments I want to store away. I want it to make me less preoccupied and more responsive to those who wait expectantly on the edges of my world.

❧

IT HAPPENED YEARS AGO on one of those raw December days that make people wish they had shopped in July. Icy winds whipped through the streets. Hunched on a sidewalk bench sat an unshaven man. He wore a threadbare jacket and shoes with no socks. He had folded a brown paper bag around his neck to keep out the biting wind.

One shopper paused, saddened by the man. *Such a pity*, she thought, wishing there was something she could do. While the shopper lingered, a little girl, eleven or twelve years old, walked by and spotted the frostbitten figure on the bench. Wrapped around the little girl's neck was a bright red woolen scarf. She stopped beside the man, unwrapped her scarf and draped it about his neck. The child walked on. The man rubbed the warm wool. And the shopper crept away, wishing she had been the one to give the scarf.

I was that shopper and I learned something that day. There is always something to give—a touch, a smile, a prayer, a kind word, a red scarf.

∽

MY DAUGHTER AND I stood beside a grandmother and a little girl whose face was sprinkled with bright red freckles. The children were waiting in line to get their cheeks painted by a local artist who was decorating them with tiger paws.

"You've got so many freckles, there's no place to paint," a boy in the line teased. Embarrassed, the girl dropped her head.

Her grandmother knelt down next to her. "I love your freckles," she said.

"Not me," the girl replied.

"Well, when I was a little girl I always wanted freckles," she said, tracing a finger across the child's cheek. "Freckles are beautiful!"

The girl looked up. "Really?"

"Of course," said the grandmother. "Why, just name me one thing that's prettier than freckles."

The little girl peered into the old woman's smiling face. "Wrinkles," she answered.

SOLITUDE

I SIT IN A BRIGHT-LIT June meadow at the Abbey of Gethsemani, a Trappist monastery in Kentucky. It is early afternoon, and I have been here since morning in what can only be described as an uneasy solitude. Time is measured here in the chant of crickets and frogs, in the syncopated litany of songbirds, in the silence of tattered wildflowers.

Even though I yearn for this acre of solitude, some other part of me hungers for the larger world of "relevance," as if my solitude were a rarefied form of loitering. By most standards, I am not being productive, efficient, or the slightest bit useful, and I can't help feeling . . . what? Extraneous? Indolent? It seems I should be writing something, cleaning something, fixing something. And I still have this tiny but stubborn repository of conditioning inside that tells me I should focus only on others, that sitting around in a monastic meadow is withdrawn, navel-gazing self-indulgence. Shouldn't I be back home working in a soup kitchen or something?

I came to the monastery because of a growing sense of alienation. Sitting here now with the heat rising in a humid vapor, I feel the intensity of it. For a while now I've wanted to put distance between myself and the world—it, and all its insufferable suffering. The world, it seems, is a ragged meadow too, maybe even a decimated one, littered with war, wounds, and wreckage, and I've felt increasingly weary of it, disengaged. Passionless in my action.

I've felt weary of people too. Incessant interaction has left me feeling a little cynical about their needs and demands. There's more hypersensitivity on my part, more resentment, less gentleness, less willingness to weave my heart with theirs in love.

Being alone in order to find the world again sounds ridiculously paradoxical. It seems so even now that I'm here. But somewhere along my spiritual journey, I'd stumbled upon a difficult and enigmatic truth: True relating is born in solitude.

As I had begun to engage in solitude I discovered and

rediscovered my essential connection to others. Over the years, it was where I unearthed the gentleness with which I could truly love others. In solitude my social consciousness had been ignited and reignited.

So once again I sit in the meadow. Despite the voice inside that tells me I'm dawdling away hours of my life, I sit in the ragged meadow, making no attempt to leave, trying to open myself to solitude's severe grace.

I reach in my backpack for my journal. Before coming here, I glued a small picture of the Tin Woodsman from *The Wizard of Oz* onto the front of it. I stare at it now. It reminds me that I'm here in search of my heart. In the original story, the Tin Woodsman is a real person whose axe becomes cursed, causing him to slowly cut away his body and his heart, piece by piece, until he is no longer covered in warm flesh, but trapped in an armor of tin. He can no longer feel or cry. His condition is numbness. His heart is lost.

I lean back on my elbows until I'm submerged in stalks of Queen Anne's lace. I close my eyes. I do not feel numb, nor is my heart really lost, and yet I resonate to the image of the Tin Woodsman. I think of the ways my heart has become distant in recent weeks. I see how I've related to those close to me with lessening intimacy, with paling shades of love, how I've looked at suffering around me and felt strangely unaffected by it. I know these things point to a heart slowly becoming lost.

I ask myself, "How did this happen?"

A flock of birds sweeps overhead in a great ceremony of sound and movement. It is one of those flocks that crosses the sky like a vast, undulating scarf, full of raucous cries. I watch until the birds are gone and then I watch the clean, gracious space they leave behind.

The birds and the sky become a contrasting metaphor that teaches me something: Lately my life has been a swarm of complexity, noise, and excess.

Left to itself, unchecked by the contemplative moment, my ego has created a small thunder of wants. I grow aware of the inner press of my thoughts, the clamor and noise they make. I'm replete with experiences, ideas, and projects— some meaningful, some trivial. I think, too, of the staggering influx of material that comes to me from news shows, weather channels, talk shows, radio programs, books, magazines, conversations. Excess comes on my fax machine, through my computer, over the phone, in the mail. I see suddenly that my life is glutted not only with activities, demands, pressures, and wants of my ego, but with data, details, news, opinions, ideas, and commentary. I read somewhere that a person today receives more information in a single edition of *The New York Times* than a person who lived a hundred years ago read in an entire year. I wonder if I am losing my inner simplicity to the age of information.

Given all this, is it any wonder there is so little space inside of me for true relating?

Solitude brings me back to a simplicity of spirit, an inner poverty that I need in order to clear room inside. It allows me to empty myself out, so there is gracious space within where I can receive myself, then God, and eventually others.

The afternoon lengthens as the sun makes its slow arc, leaving a trail of shadow across the grass. The light changes from white to deep hues of amber. The still, silent hours have begun to clear a gracious space inside me, and into this space comes presence.

The Christian mystic Hildegard wrote, "God hugs you. You are encircled by the arms of the mystery of God." I have always loved those words, and I believe it is solitude, most of all, that brings us into this circle of presence. But be forewarned: Solitude is no dainty hug. God's is a fierce embrace.

This is because solitude is an arena of transformation. Often the first thing we encounter in the gracious space that opens inside us is ourselves. We enter a realm where we can receive ourselves with unconditional presence and acceptance. Solitude allows us to confront our anger, hurt, greed, self-absorption, envy, apathy, hatred, busyness, cynicism—all the soul-fraying compulsions that keep us sequestered in our alienation.

I pick up a rock and turn it over in my hands. I am encountering things inside that I would just as soon not have to face. I look at the little circle of loamy black earth, which a moment ago was covered by the rock in my hand, at the creepy-crawly things that are wiggling in the sudden glare. "In solitude you are stripped to your nothing," a monk once told me, and sitting here, I believe him. I feel stripped of defenses and distractions, all the normal diversions that keep me blissfully unaware of just how ragged my soul really is. Weaknesses, illusions, false patterns, and painful truths rise inexorably to the surface.

Solitude becomes a descent into the labyrinths of self, where we set up a dialogue with our own depths, where we face the denied and undiscovered, the places we live falsely and cut off from others.

In the meadow of Gethsemani, I confront my own chorus of voices. I wrestle as honestly as I can with the things that cause my resistance to love, and as I do, I begin to die to them.

Solitude is the School of Death. Abba Moses, one of the desert fathers, said, "Go, sit in your cell, and your cell will teach you everything." I believe what he was really saying was: Go sit in solitude, in the School of Death, and it will teach you everything you need to know about living the spiritual life. It will teach you how to die to ego, to the patterns that keep your heart walled up, to those things inside that prevent you from planting your heart in the world.

Jesus said, to find your life, you must lose it. Dying in order to live is at the heart of the Christian faith and it is at the heart of spiritual transformation. Yet most of us are truants when it comes to the School of Death. In solitude, however, we cannot avoid it.

If we remain in our solitude without fleeing, we not only

see and wrestle with what keeps us resistant to love, we not only release the desire to hold onto these things, but we also release the struggle. We meet ourselves fully and then we let go. We let go into God.

Solitude ruptures our illusion of separateness by returning us to the source of our unity. As Anne Morrow Lindbergh observed, "Only when one is connected to one's own core is one connected to others . . . And for me, the core, the inner spring, can best be refound through solitude."

The sky over the meadow becomes a membrane of orange colors. Light is broken with the promise of dusk. But I see more clearly than I have in months: As my life became overcrowded, complex, and noisy inside, my heart responded by growing distant and distracted. I began to live under the illusion of separateness, to live as a detached ego, unaware that I was part of a vast fabric of being, of a divine and communitarian oneness.

There are ants in the meadow. I watch them now. How they move in relentless community, trekking through the dimness on their way home. Separate, but inseparable. And I am moved by the beauty of my connection to them. In some mysterious way I feel that by watching them, I am watching myself, that I am watching the presence of God.

⟋

ON THE FIRST NIGHT of our vacation I took a solitary walk on the beach. In the distance, pier lights shredded the darkness with long, yellow beams. Waves spilled loudly on the shore.

After a mile or so I sat down, and gazing into the starry night, I became aware of a great rhythm about me, as though my hand had inadvertently slipped upon a pulse beating deep in the universe. The stars wheeled in precise pattern, the moon and the tides came and went without skipping a beat, and the wind moved like a breath. Night and day, wind and tide, current and moon. It was a magnificent dance to silent music, choreographed by the Creator.

I wondered. Hadn't God designed the world within me and the world around me to be lived according to a certain rhythm and to be danced in accordance with the silent music of divine will? *When my life seems off balance, restless and fragmented, can it be that I am out of step with God?*

I stood up and began the walk back, ready once more to fix my eyes and heart on the Choreographer.

∾

I SLIP OUT INTO a star-filled summer night. Alone I look up and pretend the stars appear only once every hundred years. And tonight is the night! I begin to see the grandeur of the heavens, the sky jeweled with countless twinkling lanterns. In the timeless constellations, I see God's signature. In the night wind, I feel a touch. In the whisper of leaves, I hear a song. Just like that, my soul wakes up! Once more, for me, the universe is crammed with God.

∾

I WAS SPENDING THE AFTERNOON talking with artist Meinrad Craighead in her studio. I'd come to see her because I was drawn to the symbolic, surreal images in her paintings—images of rebirth, nourishment, creation, and nature's cycles.

Back home a print of one of her paintings hung in my study. It depicted a child sitting before a cluster of yellow irises that had sprung from the ground. The child waves her arms gracefully in front of the irises as if she's conducting an orchestra, summoning forth music from the flowers. That, it seemed to me, was what Meinrad did when she painted. She lifted her arms like a conductor and summoned beautiful, creative music from the "petaled places" inside herself.

"Where does your creativity come from?" I asked her the day of my visit. She pointed to a simple altar on the wall of her studio. "I go there every day," she said.

Today, I have a wooden altar hanging on my study wall. And outside, there's a large stone in the shade of my garden. I go to these places to pray, to listen for the music and tap what is deep and real inside me.

THE SACRED ORDINARY

WHEN I EMBARKED on my spiritual journey, I was experiencing a kind of religious burnout. I'd inherited a Protestant tradition in which I found myself doing a lot of things for God, but I starved on the inside for some sort of contemplative experience. We seemed to talk a lot about the Word of God, and what to believe, and how to act—shepherding great flocks of *shoulds* and *oughts*—but to say very little about how to grow God organically in our own soul, how to incubate the divine life, and birth God.

I went away for a retreat at a Catholic oratory and began to taste silence and solitude, to pray contemplatively, to brush against deep, intoxicating mysteries. After my first retreat, which was for me an extraordinary encounter with the inner Beloved, I came home to grocery shopping and children and bills and work and phone calls. Plain old life. It was startling in its incongruence. Here in the noise of life there was mostly God's supreme absence.

One Monday morning I drove to church. "I will go back to the silence," I told myself. The sanctuary was locked, but I finally located a housekeeper with a key. She couldn't understand what I wanted to do there on Monday. "Church was yesterday," she told me apologetically.

"I know. I just want to sit inside awhile." Why did I feel so foolish? The housekeeper's vacuum cleaner whined loudly in the corridor off the sanctuary. The stained glass beamed down on me. Maybe it was the vacuum cleaner, maybe it was me, but even the window didn't look particularly holy. Where was God? Longing rose in me.

That Monday I knew I would have to settle one thing. If I am intent on centering my life in the presence of God, then I must understand what I believe about where this presence can be found. Had I limited God's presence to what I perceived as sacred—to holy places and church-sponsored moments? Had I assumed the material world was more or less empty of God? Had I separated common things from spiritual things, and routine moments from holy moments?

What does a running vacuum cleaner have to do with God? The question seemed important, crucially important. This incident may sound small and silly, but it was a turning point. God, I realized, is not partial to stained glass.

That same afternoon I was downtown, sitting on a bench while my son played on an old cannon in front of the courthouse. I looked at the bank on the corner, and the bus stop, and the people lined up—especially at one old woman who had a blue sweater on her head, buttoned under her chin like a scarf. An ordinary, mundane slice of life. But sitting there enveloped in bus fumes and traffic sounds, I somehow situated myself in the silence of my own heart, and I remember being nearly knocked breathless by the sudden love I felt welling up in me for the lady with the sweater on her head. The whole moment was pregnant with divinity. God was the fume-laden air, and the sun slanting off the courthouse roof, and the groan of the bus, and the old woman. It was as if a veil slipped off my illusions and I saw what Is. That was the God-life breaking into the here and now. The noise became the music.

I began at that moment to heal my own deeply carved duality. God became the steam of my soup, the uprooted tree, the graffiti on the building, the rust on the fence. It was possible to have deep encounters with Absolute Reality in the midst of dealing with annoying people, or while peeling onions or cleaning rotting leaves from my downspouts with the help of complaining children. Hildegard of Bingen said, "God loves what is earthly." So true.

᠊᠊᠊

WHATEVER THE GREAT MYSTERY IS, everything that has come to be in the universe is the manifestation and a revelation of it. Everything is infused with the unspeakable and ineffable dimension of this mystery. Everything. The giraffe, the rain forest, crab grass, peat moss, rattlesnake, and human being. If the mystery is divine music, so too is the universe. The universe is one grand harmonious concert, a symphony of divine music.

∾

A TINY WAIL PIERCED the silence of the bedroom. I moved mechanically into the worn-out path from my bed to the nursery like a tired old soldier with battle fatigue. The numbers on the clock glowed green, iridescent, and grim. It was 4:02 AM . . . Mother's Day.

The little cry flung itself furiously into the darkness. It was not her hungry cry. That one had shattered the night at 2:50. This was the colic cry . . . the third one tonight. I lifted my three-month-old daughter from her crib and dropped wearily into the rocking chair, my eyelids sinking closed like iron anchors dropped to sea. She screamed into the crook of my elbow. I rocked back and forth, trying to weave time into something bearable. The creak in the chair groaned heavily. *The sound of motherhood*, I thought. My arm began to throb beneath her as sleep crept slowly into her breathing. I dared not move. Just a few more minutes . . .

"Mama! I'm thirsty," came a loud, invisible voice out of the night. I opened my eyes to an abrupt narrow slit.

Three-year-old Bob stood in the doorway like a lost shadow. He stepped closer, clutching a stuffed dinosaur.

"Go to bed and I'll bring some water in a little while." My whisper had the ragged edge of desperation.

"But I want some water now!" he halfway yelled.

The baby jerked and cranked up her cry.

I could almost hear the last gasp down inside my heart. "Now look what you did! You woke your sister. Now go to bed!" I shouted. He didn't. He stood there and added his wail to hers. It was too much. My eyes turned away, falling on the green diaper pail. Full again. I looked from it to the door. At the end of the dark hall, the den was littered with toys, pacifiers, and broken cookies. Beyond that, short and tall baby bottles lined the kitchen counter like a miniature skyline. My small world.

That's when the flame of joy that burns mysteriously inside a mother's heart simply went out. I sat in the nursery like a snuffed candle and drew the darkness around me. Actually, my despondency had been gathering for weeks. It wasn't the kind of thing I wanted to admit, but something had gradually gone out of my mothering—the sparkle, the eagerness, the delight. It had been swallowed up by an ocean of frustrations and demands. Oh, I loved my children. But lately, caring for them had become a burden. "God," I whispered, near tears myself. "I don't want to be a mother today. I'm sick of it!"

The terrible honesty startled me. How could I say that! How could I feel this way! I wondered if all mothers sometimes despaired of being mothers. Was it only me?

My husband waded into the shrieking darkness, rubbing his eyes as if he'd wakened into a real live nightmare. "What's going on?" he said.

"I'm thirsty and she don't love me," cried Bob.

The baby squalled, her red face bobbing against my shoulder like a furious woodpecker.

"Here, give the children to me," he said bravely. "You go to bed."

"They're all yours," I said, thrusting Ann into his arms.

I fell into bed, despising the way I felt.

I woke to the inevitable wail. My eyes focused on the window where the first sliver of daylight hemmed the curtain. The same sense of despondency filled my chest. I rose, dreading the day. I dreaded preparing the children for church—the bathing, feeding, dressing, redressing. Every task was like a heavy gray bead on a chain around my neck.

On the drive home from church, Bob's voice floated over the front seat. "We talked about mothers in Sunday school."

"Oh, really," I muttered.

"My teacher said I made you a mother when I was borned."

"It's *born*. Not *borned*," I corrected.

"Tell me the story of when I was borned—I mean born."

I glanced around at him, getting a whiff of the carnations pinned at my shoulder. His face was poked out with curiosity. "Not now," I said, looking away.

By mid-afternoon the sky was charcoal gray. A slow drizzle of rain washed the den windows. In a rare moment of quiet, I stood at the panes, my depression deepening.

"Mama, now will you tell me the story of when I was born?" Bob stared up at me.

I sighed and dropped onto the sofa. He climbed beside me, waiting.

"It was late one night," I began reluctantly. "Daddy and

I had waited and waited for you. We thought you never would get here. But finally you decided to come. Daddy drove me to the hospital." I paused, my heart not in the telling.

"Then I was born?" he urged me on.

"Yes. The first time I saw you, you had all your fingers in your mouth making silly noises."

He giggled. "Like this?" He stuck four fingers in his mouth and snorted.

I managed a smile.

"Did you hold me?"

"Yes, we had a long visit that night," I said. "You were wrapped in a blanket and your hair was combed up into a curl like the top of an ice cream cone."

I could almost see the hair, the small wrinkled face. It seemed like yesterday.

Outside, lightning splintered the grayness, and inside, Bob's eyes were wide and blue. I looked at the shifting streams on the window and wondered why motherhood could not have remained so fresh and golden as those first moments.

The story seemed ended. But then, a small forgotten piece of it came back to me. "I nearly forgot. There was a card tucked in your blanket that night. A card from the hospital."

"What did it say?" Bob asked, perched high on the sofa cushion. I squinted, unable to recall exactly. Suddenly I was searching our shelves, digging out his baby book. Dust sealed the pages with neglect. Bob hung over my shoulder as I ruffled through the yellowed memories.

I found the card in the back of the book. It was personalized with a slightly faded, slightly smudged inkblot of his hand. Five newly born fingers and one incredibly tiny palm. My eyes drifted over the tender little image down to the inscription beneath it . . . a simple greeting card verse:

Make the most of every day,
for time does not stand still.
One day this hand will wave good-bye
while crossing life's brave hill.

The room grew quiet. Rain trickled on the panes. Bob took the card, his fingertips moving in silent wonder along the edge of the handprint. My throat felt tight. How big his hands had become. And so quickly. His fingers were long and skinny next to the little image, his palm a baseball glove in comparison. His hand holding the tiny inkblot became a living picture of time moving, of life flowing swiftly and silently through its passages. *Make the most of every day. Time does not stand still.*

I drew Bob to me and hugged him tightly, my heart catching as that fragile flame inside seemed to ignite again.

"You're going to pop me, Mama," he said, laughing.

～

DRIVING THROUGH the poorer section of a large city, I noticed cracker-box houses wedged among the cement block tenements and billboards. There was little birdsong, few trees. Mostly it was a concrete world. Dogs without collars. Dirt without grass. Children without butterflies.

A strange restlessness began to stir in me, a bit of sadness.

At a stop sign, I paused before yet another dilapidated old house, scraped by the years of all its paint. But that's not what grasped my attention. Across the front of it was a window box with newborn red flowers tilting over the side. Tulips, I believe. An elderly woman was watering them from a tin can. She appeared to be unaware of all the concrete, of the sadness that seemed to seep through its cracks.

As I watched her, she did something so lovely, so breathtaking, I can still see it. She reached down and patted the soil around her flowers as a mother pats a sleeping child. Then she bent her face close to them and rubbed a petal against her cheek.

As I drove, I realized how deeply beauty feeds the soul, how important it is to create it in the midst of ugliness, barrenness, and sorrow. In every small famine of the spirit.

❧

ONE AFTERNOON when I was eight, I sat on the bank of a pond with my grandfather, fishing. He wore a straw hat. I wore a dandelion behind my ear. Wind lifted the pine needles, and there was not another sound—only my granddaddy's breathing. He had left work early to bring me fishing. I knew that was not easy. He was a busy man, a judge.

For a moment I forgot to watch my pole. The end splattered into the water, sending dragonflies scurrying off their lily pads. "Whoa, fishing pole," my grandfather said, reaching over to steady the cane pole, and making me giggle.

"Watch the cork," he said, his finger pointing to the water. "When our fish comes nibbling, let him have a taste, then pull."

"Yes, sir," I said.

Shadows crept over the water. The sun sank. Granddaddy sat as still as the pines, as if time were suspended and our minutes were as countless as summer berries.

I rested my cheek against his arm. "Granddaddy, are you sure there's fish in this pond?"

Now he laughed. Twilight gathered around our shoulders like an old country quilt.

Suddenly the cork zinged under the water with such force I slid down the bank. "It's a whopper!" cried Granddaddy. I dug my toes in the mud and leaned back into his arms. We pulled. Breaking through the water, erupting into the last glimmer of daylight, burst the biggest fish I had ever seen. I held up the silver fish and sucked in my breath. Granddaddy beamed. Neither of us spoke. We only stared at one another over the wiggling fish.

The gift of that afternoon was one of the best presents I ever got.

There are so many wonderful gifts I can give those I love, but the one that lingers when all the others are gone, the one that knits the brightest threads into life, is the gift of time—the gift of one's self.

ᕲ

ONE SUMMER DAY filled with the fragrance of wildflowers and waning sunlight, I was walking through an Indiana meadow when I came upon a little cemetery that belonged to the monastery perched at the top of the hill. I could not resist. I slipped through the gate and strolled among the rows of timeworn headstones, stopping now and then to read the inscriptions. One grave was still fresh, its headstone new and unweathered. Not a blade of grass grew on its neatly mounded soil.

Standing there alone in the empty quiet, I felt the inevitable reality of death intrude, the unbearable intimacy of it, and I was inhabited by a deep sadness.

As I left, I paused at the gate and looked back. Fluttering through the graveyard, dipping and dancing over the tombstones, was a small yellow butterfly. I watched it the way one watches the sun dawn or crocus bloom, reminded of the mysterious way life continually flows from death. Here in this place, it became a harbinger of hope, revealing the great round of existence: life, death, then life again.

❧

ON OUR LAST MORNING at the seashore, I stood on the balcony of our small rented cottage and took one final look at the ocean. Its vastness stretched before me, rolling on to encompass much of the earth. I had read that it contained whole mountain ranges in its depths.

As a line of pelicans swooped low over the water and dropped like a single dipper into the sea, I called back a familiar Bible verse:

If I take the wings of the morning
and dwell in the uttermost parts of the sea,
even there shall thy hand lead me
and thy right hand shall hold me.

Even there! I am sustained by the belief that God is available, at any moment, that no matter how deep or shallow my need is, I am never beyond divine guidance.

Even there. The words echo within me—on lonely days, problem days or plain ordinary days when I'm far from this beautiful sea. *Even there . . . even there.*

～

MY FRIEND ANN invited me and a few other women to her house on Saturday for "an old-fashioned bread baking," and instructed each of us to bring a cup of flour from our own kitchens. All of us were old friends, but our lives had gone in different directions. We hadn't been together in years.

That day we sifted our individual cups of flour into a single bowl. Together we dissolved the yeast, mixed and kneaded the dough, waited for it to rise, shaped it into loaf pans, then waited for it to bake. All the while we filled the warm, pungent air with talk of our mothers and grandmothers making bread, talk of how much we'd missed one another and how friendships suffered when they weren't nurtured. Finally, we pulled the loaves from the oven.

As Ann sliced a piece and handed it to me, I felt the sacredness of this day rise to fullness inside me, just as the dough had become plump and full, rising in its bowl. Through the ancient feminine art of making bread, we had rediscovered our connections with each other. And we had found that our lives, like those individual cups of flour, could be sifted together again, to form renewed relationships that nourished us inside.

❧

WHEN I WAS A CHILD, my mother and I sat on the front porch of our house in Georgia, watching the darkness creep in. Out of nowhere a mysterious yellow twinkling appeared in the night, tiny flashes of incandescence dipping beneath the pines.

"Want to catch lightning bugs?" Mother asked.

Capture that magic? Could it be done? Mother looked at my face, bounded off the steps, and fetched a Mason jar, its lid pierced with holes. We walked barefoot into the darkness, following the flickering light. Mother cupped her hands and lunged. "Look," she said, making a peephole into her hand. With my face pressed against her thumbs, I caught my first close-up glimpse of a firefly.

The jar grew full. And when Mother tucked me in that night, she placed it beside my bed. Long after everyone else was asleep, I was still wide awake watching the golden lights flare in the darkness.

Now, so many years later, I have forgotten most of the toys that filled my room. But the night Mother and I caught lightning bugs and made them into a night-light is imprinted in me.

There is so much ordinary magic dancing around the backyard waiting to be shared with someone.

❧

WE AMBLED ALONG a dusty path through the woods, toting our fishing poles to the pond. My husband and children threw themselves into the delight of fishing, but in less than a congenial mood, I grumbled about the weather, which was muggy; the fish, which weren't biting; the children, who had taken to sliding down a mud bank; and of course the fishing worms, which were . . . well, worms.

Looking for an escape, I wandered back along the same path and found my attention drawn to the footprints etched in the dust. My husband's tennis shoe, my sandal, the children's bare feet. I gazed at them attentively and thought how good it was simply to be able to walk. How wondrous to move through the woods! I noticed how our footprints mingled together in the dirt, feeling anew how precious my family is to me, how glad I am for their steps intersecting through my life. A wash of unexpected gratitude poured over me—for growing feet and the sharing of lives together.

The most significant gifts are often the ones most easily overlooked. Small, everyday blessings: woods, health, music, laughter, memories, books, family, friends, second chances, warm fireplaces, and all the footprints scattered through our days.

SIMPLICITY OF SPIRIT

I N THE ATLANTIC OCEAN a hurricane is brewing. On the weather channel the expert speaks in mantras: "hurricane of the century," "killer storm," "unprecedented storm," "bigger-than-the-state-of-Texas storm." I stand in the living room, watching as he draws an arrow on the map to show the projected impact of Hurricane Floyd. The tip of his arrow rests on Charleston, South Carolina. Charleston is my home.

It is our first hurricane experience, my husband's and mine. We batten down the house the best we can. Only once do I pause at the window, looking out at the salt marsh where the tide is flowing in, as peacefully as ever, and the egrets are going about their business obliviously. I think of the marsh grass in the early morning when the light is fogged, the way the heron stands unmoving, the water turning pink when the sun sets—and the bright largesse of living here seizes me. I feel in this moment I cannot bear what may come.

I pack two suitcases, gather the photograph albums, my grandfather's pipe, the children's baby books, the homemade Christmas tree ornaments, the small, irreplaceable things. Inside I feel daunted. When we close the door and drive away, I am struggling for composure.

We join the vast exodus, evacuating in a slow crawl inland. Yanked out of the normalcy of life, pulled into an uncommon milieu where life's transience grows vivid and everything becomes heightened and lived close to the bone, I grow aware of something unusual happening inside of me. It's as if I am being pared down like a piece of fruit, stripped, peeled, distilled to a simplicity of spirit. The events are exfoliating. They shuck me down to some place that is thick with luminosity and resilience, an enduring inner ground. What comes rising to my lips is the word *God*, and in the next breath, *home*. The whole thing is so palpable it carries an actual physical sensation.

Tears come. Not because of potential wreckage from the hurricane. They are tears about this place of presence where I've touched down, tears about the beautiful austerity of being. I do not speak for the next hundred miles.

The night after the evacuation, I fall into an unfamiliar bed and dream about *The Velveteen Rabbit*. It is about a boy and his beloved stuffed rabbit. Over the years its fur is worn off, the whiskers drop off, the tail becomes unsewn and the nose is rubbed away. It becomes threadbare, ragged with life and the rigors of love. *But*—and here's the part that made my children beg me to read the story again—the more worn down the rabbit grows, the more real it becomes. In the end it hops into the woods, fully alive, an authentic rabbit, not just a facsimile of one. The dream is the divine gift. It presents me with the process that began in me in the car: the wearing down to the real.

Whenever life bore down on a friend of mine, she would say she'd been selected for the School of Dire Truths. The hurricane experience plopped me right down in the middle of it. I learned all over again that intensely fraying events in life, like hurricanes, sometimes have a particular effect. They plunge us into a mysterious, inward divestiture, a distillation we could truly call sacred, because for a while we know—in a way that we rarely know—what matters. I mean what *really* matters. We know it utterly. And this unimpeachable knowing ushers us once again to the authentic ground that resides at the heart of life. We seem to understand—if only partially—this is the Ground of Love, the Ground of Deep Being, the Ground of Presence. It's as if the foreground of life, where we spend the majority of our time, fades away, and we are left in the great background that is God, against which all life exists.

The foreground is where we are necessarily inhabited by the stuff of life. It's the place where our souls connect with the world. The dog that sleeps at our feet, the child whose nose we wipe, the popcorn at the movie, the wind in the Spanish moss, the bowl of January camellias. The foreground is all of these, though it has its annoying spaces, as well—like the dentist's bill and the broken garage door, the arthritic knee and the long line at the hardware store.

I relish the foreground, for it is a grand playground for my soul that sometimes dazzles me with the immanence of

God. But life is not merely a one-dimensional existence in the foreground.

The unseen life is the divine background—enormous, hidden, and near—a place where our spirits connect and are touched by the Eternal.

The day of the hurricane evacuation I discovered that coming to rest at this place seems to require a distillation. It may come through the shearing experience of trial. Or, it may come through the practice of a spiritual discipline, which day after day wears a rut into the foreground, breaking through into the radiance hidden behind and beneath it. Either way, we are wearing down to the Real.

∽

MY HUSBAND'S GRANDMOTHER, Beatrice, had just finished sewing a rosebud pink dress. As she held it up for me to see, I thought about the interminable hours she must have spent pedaling her ancient sewing machine. "It's beautiful," I told her.

"Tomorrow I'll wear it to church," she announced, draping the dress over the ironing board. The iron was old and overheated. In seconds a large brown scorch seared into the skirt.

With a sigh, Beatrice pulled out her scissors and cut the dress into small squares. She tucked the little pile of squares into her sewing basket. I knew she meant them for a quilt.

On cold nights, when I draw up the quilt of rosebud pink squares that warms my bed, I sometimes think about the little pile of disappointments that I've stored away and how I can patch them together into something new.

∽

THERE WAS A WEARY TIME in my life when I was the kind of person who would go to the dog pound to leave a stray and end up taking three dogs home. I did not know how to say the word *no*. Naturally, my phone rang off the wall with requests. Would I lick one thousand envelopes for the League of Women's Voters? Would I make two life-sized, glow-in-the-dark monsters for the Halloween carnival? Seriously. Would I make two hundred cookies for the bazaar?

One day the president of the Women's Club called. "Sue, there's a new family in town. Would you make a little welcome dinner and carry it over tonight?" I worked in the kitchen all afternoon and delivered a magnificent meal across town to the family. My own family got chicken noodle soup from the can and I fell into bed, exhausted. At midnight my son woke me up, not for a glass of water, but for a peanut butter sandwich!

Needless to say, this fairly embarrassing experience had a reforming effect on me! I made a list of my priorities and discovered I was spending far too much time on things at the bottom of the list. I learned one of the most transforming lessons of my life.

Sometimes, in order to say yes to what matters most, I must say no to good things.

∽

WHILE DRIVING THROUGH the mountains of North Carolina, returning from an appointment, I felt hurried, pressured by all the "important stuff" waiting back home for my attention. Spotting a car stopped in the road ahead of me, I braked behind it, fuming a little, wondering what the problem could be. Then I saw one of those huge, silent turtles crossing the road at an unbearably slow pace. So there we sat, waiting for this creature to pass.

I observed it casually at first, then with great and particular care, reflecting upon its movements and then upon my own. Why was I racing through life at breakneck speed? I looked from the turtle to the sweep of mountains in the distance, to the rich colors of the trees. Rolling down the car window, I felt the breeze of autumn lift my hair. I sniffed mountain laurel. In that moment of simple quiescence, I tasted the beauty of life. I felt God's contemplative peace enter my heart.

It's easy to operate under the illusion that what we are doing is so important we cannot stop doing it. We think we cannot slow down, especially for something so trifling as a turtle. But that is exactly the sort of thing we must never be too busy for. Stopping is a spiritual art. It is the refuge where we drink life in.

∿

MANY OF MY CHILDHOOD MEMORIES come from the times I spent on my grandfather's farm in Georgia. I especially recall the day he gave in to my begging and let me pick cotton. I was seven, and the burlap sack I was given to collect cotton in was bigger than I was.

The cotton field stretched endlessly ahead of me freckled with white and drenched with heat. The pickers were paid by the pound, and their hands moved swiftly. They skinned the bushes of their fluffy white balls leaving me far behind. I wanted to quit. Frustrated and tearful, I looked back for my grandfather's truck and realized he was gone, having left me in the care of the field workers. Noticing my distress, a black woman idled over, her hair tied in a faded red bandana. "Mind if I pick with you?" she asked.

"No, ma'am," I said. "I don't guess so."

Her fingers worked like music along the row, and every time she dropped a handful of cotton in her sack, she dropped one in mine too. "One for you and one for me," she said.

My bag grew plump. When we took a break in the plum tree shade at the fence, I asked her why she was putting cotton in my sack.

She laughed. "For every handful you take in life, that means you've got one to give," she said.

Later she would come to work in my grandmother's house, where I would hear her repeat this incantation many times. There is brilliance in it. Imagine a world with a handful of giving for every handful of taking.

∽

ALBERT EINSTEIN WAS NOT ONLY a scientific genius, a Nobel Prize winner, and the father of the theory of relativity—he was also a man of great simplicity. One evening at a dinner party given in his honor by the president of Swarthmore College, Einstein was called upon for a speech.

He greeted the guests politely, then paused for a moment. "Ladies and gentlemen, I am sorry but I have nothing to say." As he sat down, he added, "In case I do have something to say, I'll come back."

Six months went by and one day Einstein wired the president of the college, announcing, "Now I have something to say." Another dinner was arranged and Einstein made his speech.

I love that story. It reminds me that when I speak

without forethought or restraint just to fill up silent spaces, I am only littering the air.

Enough said. . . .

❧

ONE DECEMBER when my daughter Ann was six, she tucked two gifts beneath the Christmas tree, one for her daddy, the other for me. "What do you suppose they are?" I asked my husband. He shrugged, as puzzled as I.

On Christmas morning I opened my gift to find a pair of slightly familiar-looking silver earrings. In her daddy's package was a navy tie with little tan ducks on it.

"Why, Ann," I exclaimed, genuinely amazed. "Where did you get these lovely gifts?"

"The cedar chest," she answered.

That's when I recognized the earrings as a pair I'd retired to the chest at least ten years before. The tie had been discarded long ago too. Ann had given us gifts we already possessed!

The incident caused me to consider how much my life was quietly caught in wanting, seeking, and acquisition. That trinity of all-American pursuits not only undermined my sense of what is enough, but seduced me into an artificial sense of discontent. Thanks to a six-year-old, I discovered the clean, simple wisdom of waking up to what I already have.

GRACIOUS SPACE

A NON-SOUTHERN FRIEND recently referred to me as an "un-Southern Southerner" because I don't eat grits, listen to country music, or have a football-playing brother with three first names.

His comment reminded me all over again that the South is not only a place on the map, but it's also a region in the mind, viewed through a fog of stereotypes and caricatures. On my friend's mental map, the South is apparently a Gothic realm of the picturesque and conspicuous—lazy good old boys, patriotic beauty queens, fat and corrupt sheriffs, God-and-country politicians, revival preachers, demure belles, and white-trash vixens. He was imposing the Southern catch-22: If you fail to conform to the stereotypes, people stop thinking of you as Southern.

I was raised in a tiny town tucked in the pinelands and red fields of southwest Georgia. "A beautiful nowhere," my college roommate called it when she visited.

For me, though, it's an enduring somewhere, a long-suffering lap of Southern life. It's there, where my parents still live on the same farm that my great-great-grandparents settled, that memory leans heavy against my heart. . . .

My grandmother walks about the dining room, setting a "test table," turning knife blades the wrong direction, placing iced-tea spoons where soup spoons should be, purposely committing an array of table-setting atrocities so subtle the queen of England couldn't spot them. I am twelve and my job is to do what the queen cannot. A half hour later I have triumphed, except for the individual saltcellars, which are missing their tiny spoons.

"You are Emily's Post-er child," Grandmother tells me.

For me the memory goes beyond the tattered stereotype of genteel belles. It whispers something historically Southern: decorum.

The word *decorum* comes form the root *décor*, which

means beauty, and that has long been romanticized in the South, whether at the table, on the page or, most important, in the soul. The South was considered a bastion of politeness and civility. "Mind your manners" was a Southern mantra offered to us children with the religiosity of a Tibetan chant. You could do serious time in your room for failing to say ma'am or sir, and you could dine on Ivory soap for blurting out something crude.

The decorum we have in the South today may only be a residue of an earlier time, but it persists as part of the cultural standard. And while it's true that harsh and unpleasant things need to be said at times, in most of the South, decorum would insist it be done with grace and manners, or at the very least, charm. In the South, we have a way of expressing harsh thoughts with a twist of sympathy. They tack on the words, "Bless her heart."

For example: "That is the meanest, most boorish woman I ever came upon. Bless her heart."

Back home, where people routinely bless one another's hearts, I remember not only the dining room test table, but also the pond where the cows come to drink.

My grandfather sits in a folding chair, holding his fishing pole over the water, a crooked silhouette in the last traces of daylight. He wears a gray fedora and white shirt with a tie, having come straight from the courthouse, where he's the city court judge. He doesn't consort with his pocket watch, which is his usual habit, because right now there is no time, no sense of life moving past us.

He watches the light fade on the water and doesn't seem to get a nibble. Eight years old, playing in the front seat of his truck, I come upon his cricket box. I rush it to him, inquiring how he fished all this time without bait. He smiles and makes his confession, a Southern Zen riddle I would puzzle over for years. "Today it's not the fish I'm after," he says. "It's the fishing."

On the surface such a story might reflect a stereotype of Southern laziness. But there's something else to be gleaned here: the ability to exercise what Wordsworth called "a wise passiveness." I think my grandfather understood that sometimes one makes the deepest progress sitting still, that it's not always the conquest that matters most, but being present in the moment and reflecting on the nature of things.

In a world of increasing diversity, surely decorum and

deep civility will smooth the way. As will knowing an unhurried place to rest from thoughts of acquisition and to find again Grandfather's pleasure in watching a pond become a membrane of light.

❧

THOMAS MERTON, THE TRAPPIST MONK, was quite good with a camera and often photographed the simple beauty of the Kentucky hills around his monastery.

One day he sent a photograph to a friend with this inscription: "The only known photograph of God." The color snapshot showed gentle hills under a vast blue sky. At the top of the picture, dominating the scene, was an immense sky hook, the kind used in construction to lift heavy objects. It looked like a gigantic fishhook suspended from heaven.

Our internalized images of what God is like—for instance, whether we see the Divine as distant or near, punitive or forgiving—has an immense impact on the way we experience life. For Merton, the image of a hook dangling over the world reflected his experience of a God who is driven by love to capture the human heart. This has been my experience too. The mysterious hook resonated in me as a hunger, a restlessness, or a quiet emptiness.

I have found joy in being caught.

❧

I SLIP OUT OF BED, pull on my goose-down robe and step out onto the porch of our vacation chalet in the Blue Ridge Mountains. Snowflakes fall through the darkness, molding the world into a clean white silence. Across the valley, snow is powdering the mountain, wiping away old markings and blemishes. It strikes me as a merciful exoneration.

I have ventured out here to watch the dawn. I sit in an Adirondack chair as the pink light comes, slowly climbing the back side of the mountain. As the fiery rim of the sun crests the peak and a corona of light shatters the darkness, I rise to my feet.

I have read an anonymous saying sometimes attributed to the Eskimos: "There is only one great thing, the only thing. To live to see the great day that dawns and the light that fills the world."

So it is.

∿

AS MY FRIEND BETTY AND I strolled around some plantation grounds in South Carolina, we found a trail leading off into the woods. It curved beneath moss-draped oaks that formed Gothic arches over our heads. The air floated in birdsong and silence, heavily perfumed with honeysuckle. Now and then we spotted a wild dogwood tree, its white blooms catching the light and shimmering through the dense green thicket.

"I feel like we are walking in a cathedral," I whispered.

"Aren't we?" Betty said.

We paused to admire a tuft of bridal wreath growing along the trail's edge, and that's when she came—a black butterfly with a latticework of orange and blue on her wings. She lit on the toe of Betty's shoe and to our utter surprise began to crawl up her slacks and blouse—all the way to the top of Betty's blond head.

Then, astonishingly, she flew to the top of my head and poised there for several moments before beginning a slow descent to my shoulder, then to the crook of my elbow. Not wanting to break the spell by speaking, Betty and I exchanged bemused glances. *What's going on?*

The butterfly wound down to the laces of my tennis shoe. On impulse I bent over and held my finger out to her the way you might offer it to a parakeet. The butterfly hopped right on. I lifted my finger until she was level with my nose.

I'd never been eye-to-eye with a butterfly before. It was as if I saw her through a magnifying glass—the large black hemispheres of her eyes, two tufts on either side of her mouth clothed in fuzzy hairs, and the slender proboscis with which she drank the nectar of the woods. I know this will sound strange, but her gaze seemed fixed on me, as if she were as enthralled by me as I was by her. "Hello," I said softly.

We continued on through the woods together—Betty and I, and this butterfly who rode along on my finger, and who for reasons we could not begin to fathom, seemed to be adopting us as her companions.

Finally Betty and I sat down on the ground in a clearing with our unlikely friend. She fluttered to Betty's shoulder, then back to my lap, where she performed graceful pirouettes across my kneecaps. She flitted about our heads, lit in our hair, and once she hung from Betty's earlobe like an earring.

Just when I thought she could amaze me no more, the butterfly flew to the crook of my neck and nestled there like a baby chick burrowing for protection beneath its mother's wing. As the butterfly opened and closed her wings, they grazed my throat like the brush of a baby's eyelashes, soft and barely perceptible, yet the vibration seemed to pulse through me. It felt a little like waking up. I remember a sense of ignition inside, of being engulfed by a feeling of deep connection not only with the creature at my neck, but with the whole natural world.

Later, when I had time to really think about it, I realized that I had been locked in a certain human egotism that pervades our culture. I did not seem to understand that the butterfly and I came from the same stuff of life and were linked beyond my wildest imaginings. I was suffering from a subtle estrangement from the earth. I had forgotten the depth of my kinship with it.

Such awakenings seem to come through deep encounters with the self, through the medium of heart and soul. I have heard it told that when Beethoven played his "Moonlight Sonata" at a house concert for the first time, someone came up afterward and asked, "What does this music mean?"

"I'll tell you what it means," Beethoven said. Then he sat down and played it again. Beethoven was saying what all poets know, that you arrive at the meaning of the music through an experience of the music, not an analysis of it. Likewise, I arrived at my own form of eco-spiritual awareness not by funneling facts and information about the despoliation of the earth into my head (though I'm sure that wouldn't hurt), but by listening to the "Moonlight Sonata" of a butterfly. In such ways, the poetry of creation enters us and we are changed.

∞

ONE CLOUDY AFTERNOON while driving to an appointment, I stopped at an intersection. Two elderly men stepped into the crosswalk in front of me. The tall man wore an overcoat, while the shorter one had on only a sweater. As little pellets of rain began to fly in the wind, the tall man unbuttoned his coat and held out the side so that the smaller man could squeeze inside it next to him. The two of them made their way across the street tucked together beneath one coat.

All day I could not stop thinking how it reflected the essence of friendship: the "unbuttoning" of oneself that invites intimacy, followed by the ability to step into that close, vulnerable space.

⟁

WHILE TRAVELING IN ENGLAND, my husband and I set out to find the Chalice Well. It was not mentioned on our tourist maps, but we knew it was located in a garden in the town of Glastonbury.

According to the legend, Joseph of Arimathea, who took the body of Jesus down from the cross, came to Glastonbury in AD 37, bringing with him the Holy Grail—the chalice Jesus drank from at the Last Supper. This lost grail has inspired countless quests throughout the world. For twenty centuries myths have persisted that he buried it inside the Chalice Well.

In Glastonbury we found a garden on Chilkwell Street that seemed to be the place. The custodian was an elderly lady with white hair and eyes the color of wood hyacinths. She directed us to a garden path.

It was a little like stepping into a Monet painting. We wound past lily pools and banks of flowers that blurred into blue mist. A man wearing a tweed coat sat on a bench lost in thought. Farther along, a woman leaned against a rose arbor, meditating in silence.

The path ended abruptly at a well, which was covered with a wrought iron lid decorated with an image known as the *vesica pisces*, or vessel of the fish, which is an ancient anagram referring to Jesus. As I gazed at it, I couldn't help but wonder if maybe the legend could be true.

I was still pondering the possibility as we retraced our steps through the garden. At the gate, I paused and asked the custodian, "Do you believe the legend?"

"Every day people come from all over the world to this spot, looking for the cup of Christ," she said. "Whether it is here or not, doesn't matter. What matters is seeking it inside your own hearts."

She reminded me that the thirst for God is a deep and mysterious thing, which we often try to quench by searching in far-flung places. Ultimately, though, spiritual refreshment is found close to home, in the wellsprings of our own being.

✐

I WAS AWAKENED by a crash of thunder. A torrent of rain slammed against the beach house and lightning filled the room with stuttering light. I lay awake listening to the violent roar of the waves. Finally, near dawn the storm abated.

After breakfast I walked down to the beach to discover the shore strewn with beauty: uncommon shells that had been stirred up from the ocean floor, sea-polished pieces of driftwood, rumpled chains of seaweed. I bent down and picked up a Junonia. I had collected shells all my life, but this was the first one I'd ever found.

I carried the speckled pink shell back to the cottage—a reminder that in every squall there is a gift, in every upheaval a redemptive moment.

✐

AFTER YEARS OF HARBORING a secret desire to paint, I signed up for a watercolor class. At the first session, the instructor demonstrated painting a landscape, pointing out that a watercolor is created by building up one layer of color on top of another.

He brushed on the first layer, a wash of cobalt blue, then leaned back in his chair.

Silence settled over the room. I stared at my shoes, while the student next to me repeatedly cleared her throat. The moment lengthened, this unnerving, unexplained waste of time. What was he doing? Finally the teacher dipped his brush back into the cobalt blue and painted another layer. "The most common mistake by novice painters," he said, "is that they are so anxious to get to the finished result they don't take time to let one layer dry before adding another one. Creating art requires patience and waiting."

The implication extends far beyond painting a watercolor. Surely the greatest work of art any of us can ever create is our own soul. In the slow, delicate layering, there are necessary places of waiting, incubation, and integration. Within these things lies the holiness of non-doing.

SEVERE GRACE

G OD CALLS US throughout our life to severe grace, the grace of the cocoon.

We are called to separate from the old, to die in order to be born. If we open ourselves to this severe grace, we encounter God in new places: in the cyclone, in the dark, in the crisis that shatters our old confining consciousness. It is this severity that makes us new.

LAST YEAR I VISITED a woman in the hospital who is a poet and deeply contemplative. She was in a lot of pain from crippling arthritis, but she said with confounding vibrancy, "Today I have discovered God as the awful throbbing in my joints. God is the pitiful crying of the woman in the next bed. God is my loneliness. God is the angry nurse who avoids me. I did not expect God to be these things. But here in the hospital before all these agonies, I keep wanting to drop to my knees. Do you think I'm strange?"

"No," I said. "Not strange. Blessed."

✺

DID YOU KNOW THAT grain seeds that had lain for thousands of years in the pyramids of Egypt sprouted after being planted? Not only that, weed seeds recovered from the sunken Spanish galleon *Atocha* sprouted after three hundred fifty years in salt water! Seeds, I learned, no matter how old, are alive. Dormant but still alive. When the right conditions come along—the right amount of warmth or soil or moisture— they wake up and bloom.

While reading Thoreau's *Walden*, I happened upon a similar story:

There was a table made of applewood, which stood in a farmer's kitchen in New England for sixty years. One day a gnawing sound began to emanate from the table. It kept up for several weeks, until at last a bug emerged from the table, unfurled its wings and took flight.

An insect egg had been deposited in the trunk of the apple tree before it was made into a table and had remained in the wood all those years. Warmed, perhaps by the heat of a coffee urn placed on the table, it hatched, and the little bug gnawed its way out.

Who knows what unhatched potential—what dormant seeds—lie in our lives?

We are seeded with hidden promise.

❧

MY LOCAL NEWSPAPER carried a picture of a house with a caved-in roof. The living room was waist-high with snow. It covered the sofa, the chairs, and tables. The caption read, "Roof gives way under weeks of accumulated snow." The owner had let the drifts pile up till it all came tumbling down at once.

It is easy to be critical of this kind of negligence, but I've done the same thing with anger. Storing it up in bits and pieces—a few silent irritations here, some inward resentments there—until I have an overloaded roof ready to cave in on someone.

There is both spiritual and psychological wisdom in the adage, "Don't let the sun go down on your anger." I made a promise to myself to shovel it daily.

〜

SOMETIMES AT NIGHT when I wake up thirsty or sometimes on August afternoons when I walk barefoot on hot, cracked earth, I remember the African girl seeking water. She came out of nowhere, a small thirsty child.

It was 1975. My husband and I were living in East Africa. Drought had seared the plains that stretched beyond our rented farmhouse. Rivers had turned to dust, corn had dried away, and people wandered in search of water. I saw the girl from my car. She was hunched on her knees in a dry riverbed. As I drew closer, I saw that she was digging. Her small black hands scraped out a hole, hoping for a puddle of dirty water to fill her gourd. "How far have you come?" I asked her in Swahili.

"Five miles. The wells are all empty." I was amazed by the

distance she'd walked. All my life, water was something that flowed magically into my house by twisting my wrist, something I washed my car in, something I took for granted.

I handed her my canteen, which brimmed with fresh, clean water, and she turned it up and drank deeply. "*Asante, asante*," she said. Thank you. Thank you.

The encounter brought to mind the words of Jesus: "I am living water." With exploding new clarity, I realized what faith in God meant to a parched, dying life, to someone roaming and digging in dusty places for hope. The spiritual life is an endless river, a bottomless spring, a deep well.

WE STOOD ON THE ROTTEN STEPS of a crumbling house in our prim public health blue, clutching our nurses' black bags. We had come to see Juan. He was seven, a reluctant fellow desperately in need of immunizations. I was all of twenty-two years old, newly graduated. A complete novice. On my last visit Juan had refused to let me touch him. So this time I had brought Maggie, the veteran.

Juan's dark, suspicious eyes peered at us from the doorway. In his hand was the grimiest bologna sandwich I had ever seen.

"Hello, Juan," Maggie said.

He stared at her glumly and took a bite of that filthy sandwich that looked as if it had been fished out of a mud puddle.

Maggie knelt beside him and said, "I sure am hungry." Juan gave her an uncertain look. "I really like bologna," she said. He studied his half-eaten sandwich and slowly, hesitantly, held it out to her. She took a bite. A big bite. With that hard ball of bread and bologna and dirt in her mouth, she looked positively humble. Juan flashed her a smile, then he held out his arm and became immune to some pretty terrible diseases.

Maggie taught me that often the best way to reach someone on the other side of an invisible wall is to stoop under it.

❧

ONCE I PRAYED for patience. The next day my washing machine broke down, leaving me with three dozen dirty cloth diapers. Then, so help me, the dryer quit working five minutes after a monsoon started!

That day I was reminded of something that C. R. Findley once observed: God doesn't always answer prayer as we expect. Sometimes when we pray for a certain virtue—like patience—God does not necessarily send it to us in a package ready for instant use. We are much more likely to be put in a situation where we are given the opportunity to *develop* that virtue.

I am more patient today than I was before I washed thirty-six diapers by hand in a bathtub and hung them to dry from the chandeliers.

∽

I STROLLED ALONG A TRAIL in the Kentucky woods, unsure where it led. I had been walking quite awhile when I came upon a huge bronze sculpture of two men sleeping. It was an exquisite work of art. How had it come to be in the middle of hundreds of wooded acres in rural Kentucky? I circled it, gradually realizing that it was a depiction of two of Christ's disciples sleeping in the Garden of Gethsemane.

When I resumed my walk, I quickly stumbled upon

another life-sized bronze, this one quite obviously Christ in agony on his knees—a depiction of his suffering in the garden. Surrounded by the hush of the woods, I was moved by the lonely solitude of Jesus. I sat on the ground, watching sunlight fleck across the dark surface of the sculpture. It brought to mind the woman at Hiroshima whose shadow was scorched into a wall, Jews in concentration camps, Africans in slavery, the missing and murdered, abused children—the interminable suffering world.

Later, when I passed back by the statue of the sleeping disciples, I was forced to think of the apathy that contributed to the suffering. I was forced to think of how I slept.

MY LITTLE BROTHER WADE and I were playing hide-and-seek. He was hiding, I was seeking. After searching for a long time, I heard frantic, muffled cries coming from the bathroom. Finding the door locked, I hurried to tell my mother. She grabbed a kitchen chair and dragged it outside across the grass where she positioned it under the bathroom window and climbed up.

"The window screen is locked," Mother said, desperation edging into her voice.

As the strangled sound of my brother's cry filtered through the window, my mother, an average-sized woman, tore the sealed screen right off the window frame with her bare hands, and wrenched open a steel lock. She climbed through the window and found my brother stuck inside the clothes hamper.

The memory of my mother standing on the chair beneath the bathroom window has never left me. It reassures me that when the time comes, I will have the resources I need in order to cope. Something in us rises up to meet the moment.

ᥱ

ONE SPRING DURING ROUTINE SURGERY, my husband lost his voice. He woke up from anesthesia speaking in a raspy whisper. We were told the laryngeal nerve had been cut. The damage was permanent and irreparable. I still remember the cold, numbing shock I felt. My husband was thirty years old, a college teacher, a chaplain.

For months, every time I watched him struggle to be understood, I would ask God for a miracle. Every time I saw him unable to call the children in from play or unable to sing his silly songs, I would ask again.

A year passed. I prayed, but there was no miracle. His voice did not return.

Still struggling to accept what had happened, I opened the mail one morning to find a letter from a college teacher whom I'd not heard from in eight years. Out fell an orange sticker, as small as a postage stamp. On it was a gull, its wings spread in flight across the sky, and these words, "There is a miracle inside you."

It caused me to remember the lines in the Serenity Prayer: "God, grant me to accept the things I cannot change, the courage to change the things I can, and the wisdom to know the difference."

The miracle we found was acceptance.

❧

IT WAS SCARCELY MIDAFTERNOON, yet the doctor's waiting room was dark. Outside, enormous black clouds roiled and rolled. A storm was on the way. From my green chair in the corner, I felt strangely part of it—the peculiar darkness, the impending storm. I'd come here because of a lump in my breast. I'd discovered it myself, and naturally I'd gone to the family doctor hoping he would pat my hand and say, "Nothing to it." Instead, he'd sent me here, to a surgeon.

Lump. I turned the word over in my mind. It always rang the same ominous note, striking a particular chord buried years before when I'd worked as a nurse. It was a memory I never tampered with. Now it came back.

Mrs. Holly was literally the first patient I ever had. She'd had a lump, one that began her long battle with cancer. I cared for her for weeks. In all that time she never had a visitor. One morning as I brought her breakfast tray, I found her leaning at the window. Against the breaking light her frail silhouette reminded me of the dark contours of pain and longing that seemed to shape so much of her life. "Where is God?" she asked, gazing into the distance.

"Right here with us," I replied, serving up the answer almost as easily as her meal.

She turned and looked at me intently. "I wonder," she

whispered. At that moment I felt nearly as lost and unconvinced as she did. We never spoke of it again, but the episode always hung unfinished between us like a puzzle you can't solve or a book you never complete.

I sat by her bed as she died. There were just the two of us. I kept thinking about the question she'd asked that day. Maybe it was my imagination, but I felt she was thinking of it too. She was too weak to talk, but near the end she gave me a faint smile. Then she closed her eyes and died. I had never seen anyone die. It was stunning in its finality. That last caving breath extrapolated her question: Where is God? I didn't know the answer. I honestly didn't know. And I did not know how to bear the doubt.

I felt unsettled for weeks afterward. Sometimes my eyes mysteriously filled with tears when I passed her room. "I know she was your first patient," a colleague said. "But you can't get emotionally involved like this." I took her advice. I packed up the hurt, the unanswerable question and buried it. All that remained of the experience was the small dread that twisted in my stomach at every mention of the word *lump*.

The nurse's words cut through my thoughts, "Mrs. Kidd,

the doctor will see you." I followed her, trying to shake the disquieting memory.

After the exam the surgeon cleared his throat. "We need to take out the lump and get a biopsy," he said.

"Do you think it could be malignant?" I asked.

He smiled. "Most lumps turn out to be benign and I think it's entirely probable yours will be also. But you know I can't make absolute promises."

Surgery was set. I would check into the hospital in a few days.

As I pulled into the driveway at home, the first drops of rain broke from the swollen skies. I spotted my son in the backyard pulling his bicycle out of the rain. "Hurry, it's already coming down!" I yelled.

Bob bumped his wheels over the roots of the oak tree, scaring up a chipmunk that lived in the woodpile. "Will the storm hurt the chipmunks?" he asked.

"They'll be okay."

"How about them?" He looked up to the crook of an oak limb, at a bird's nest that he'd discovered the week before.

My life was imploding and he was standing in the rain

worrying about birds and chipmunks. "Yes, the entire animal kingdom will be fine!" I practically shouted, "Now come on!"

The incongruity continued all evening—the collision of small inconsequential details and the uncertainty of life, of God.

While everyone was asleep, I tossed on my pillow, listening to the rain pound the roof. Raveled in my thoughts and fears were images of Mrs. Holly.

Not wanting to wake my husband, I wandered to the den, where I sank into a chair. Lightning irradiated the panes with light, illuminating the backyard. For an instant I glimpsed the oak branches pitching and swaying in the night. I drew my knees beneath my chin and listened to the wind slap like helicopter blades in the blackness. "Where is God?" Only this time it was no longer an echo lost in the years between us. It was my own question.

I was startled to realize how abandoned I'd felt since discovering the lump. It wasn't just facing this uncertainty that seemed so fearful; it was facing it alone, without my faith. *Where were you when Mrs. Holly looked for you? How do I know you're real? That you care?* I felt relief saying it. I went back to bed lighter, as if a clean new space had been created inside me.

The next morning a bit of sunshine dribbled over a cloud. The children scurried out to play. It wasn't long before shouts erupted from the backyard. "Mama! Mama!"

I leaped a row of puddles. Beneath the oak, at the tips of the children's tennis shoes, lay the bird's nest. Sprawled beside it were two baby birds. They groped in the grass, looking helpless and wet. "They fell from the tree!" cried Bob. "And you said they'd be okay. You said—"

"I know," I interrupted, remembering how the branches had lashed about in the wind.

As I scooped the hatchlings into my hands and placed them in the nest, a fragment of an old familiar Bible verse came to me:

Consider the birds of the air . . .
One of them shall not fall on the ground
without your Father.

I held the words in my mind and felt them descend slowly into my heart—into that clean, new space.

I tucked the nest into the ivy that draped the brick fence, while the children agonized over whether the mother bird would find it. The next day, however, she appeared on the fence with a beak full of food. The birds were fine.

And I was too. The lump was benign.

Gradually, the memory of Mrs. Holly healed inside me. I want to believe she found the assurance of God's presence before she died.

I found it through honesty, through faith, through choice.

∾

THIS OLD HASIDIC STORY is one of my favorites.

A rabbi asked his students a question. "When does night end and day begin?"

"Is it the moment you can see the difference between an olive tree and a fig tree?" one student asked.

"No," said the rabbi. "That's not it."

"Is it the moment you can tell the difference between a sheep and a dog?" asked another.

The rabbi shook his head. "No, that's not it either.

Rather, it is the moment you look at the face of a stranger and recognize that it is really the face of your brother."

✺

WHEN I VISITED ISRAEL in 1980, I walked through the Garden of Gethsemane at dusk, pausing beside the gnarled trunk of an olive tree. As the tour guide recited the story of the night Jesus had slipped into the garden and grappled with his suffering, I noticed a thorny vine growing at the base of the tree. The guide identified it as the Crown of Thorns.

I stooped down and touched my finger to a thorn. As I did, I noticed something I'd almost missed. A vibrant red bloom grew from the stem.

That was the image from the trip that haunted me long after I returned home: the fiery red flower on the crown of thorns.

Every suffering has its eruption of beauty and life.

✺

IT IS EARLY AFTERNOON as I step through the cold clumps of fog to my grandparents' house. I am home from college for the Christmas holidays, eager to see my grandfather, who has become ill and weak while I was away. Recently he has been confined to a wheelchair.

I turn and wave to my father as he drives away, headed for the farm he and my grandfather have tended for a lifetime.

The five hundred acres of land have been in the Monk family since the early 1800s, passed down from generation to generation. My great-grandparents, William and Alcy, are buried here. My grandfather does not just love the land, he reverences it. He knows every row of corn, every spindle-leg calf, every seedling pine. The farm is the crucible of his childhood, the place his soul understands as home.

"Merry Christmas, Granddaddy," I say, walking into the room my grandmother calls the parlor.

He looks up from his wheelchair and smiles, his eyes faded and watery. "How's my girl?" It is the way he says it that pierces me, the same way he said it when I was six and ten and fourteen. I am his girl. I have always been his girl.

A chill winter rain begins to sift through the grayness at the window as I try to strike up a cheery conversation, first about my college courses, and then the weather. He listens, but my words wander into little cul-de-sacs. He sits there and sadness rises up. We end up listening to the rain.

"The rain will do the farm good," Granddaddy says suddenly.

I sit straight up and know that it's the farm that fills his eyes with such longing. For weeks now he has been too weak to make the seven-mile trip.

He pulls out his pocket watch. "I imagine the cows are feeding now. They'll be in the front pasture now, bunched under the pines like they do on wet days."

"You miss the farm," I say.

"I miss it," he responds and looks away so I cannot see how much.

The afternoon darkens. I put on the lamp and settle back in the chair while Granddaddy nods with sleep. He wakes as my father stomps across the porch. The front door opens.

"I'm back," he calls, and appears in the doorway holding a tiny pine tree. It is three feet tall, shimmering with crystals of rain and tied all over with small red velvet bows. My father stands the radiant little tree at the window.

"You know that stand of pines in the front pasture?" he says, "I was there feeding the cows. They were huddled there under the trees. I looked down by the fence and saw this pine growing, and somehow I thought it would make a nice Christmas tree."

I wheel my grandfather over so he can touch the needles. I watch how his eyes fill up—the only tears I've ever seen him cry. How he smiles through them. How Christmas shines around us.

A TASTE OF SILENCE

OFTEN I FEEL like that famous contemplative, Charlie Brown. My favorite Charlie Brown story is about the time he and Lucy were sailing on a cruise ship. Lucy, great philosopher that she is, said, "You know, Charlie Brown, life is like a cruise ship. Some people take their deck chairs to the back of the ship to see where they have been. And some people take their deck chairs to the front of the ship to see where they are going. What kind of person are you, Charlie Brown?" He pauses reflectively, and then says, "I'm the kind of person who can't get my deck chair open." In the contemplative life, I'm still trying to open my deck chair.

Somehow, as a young woman with a husband, two children, a station wagon, a dog, a demanding career, a busy social life, and endless church activities, I stumbled headlong upon a contemplative path. It was very disconcerting.

I embarked on my immense journey, quite timidly, hip-deep in American life. I began to read the contemplative literature, moving through volumes of Western spiritual classics, finding particular heroes in St. Teresa, John of the Cross, Julian of Norwich, Meister Eckhart, Hildegard of Bingen, the anonymous author of *The Cloud of Unknowing*, and most especially, Thomas Merton, whose work became a wise and provocative mentor.

I began to meditate and to make regular monastic retreats. My friends could not imagine what insanity had gotten into me. "What ever are you doing, going to those places?" a friend asked with unveiled concern in her voice.

"I can't help it," I told her. "After all, my middle name is Monk." I suppose this was my way of avoiding a real answer.

The truth is that there is a "monk" who lives in me, an archetypal monk whom I must honor and allow to be. This monk craves the depths of solitude and silence and has, at times, a searing passion for God and an almost raging empathy for creation. She is the part of me that wants to come out in cataphatic celebration—dancing, writing, and painting my spiritual journey. She is also the part of me that wants to enter the apophatic darkness of no-thing. I love the monk who lives in me very much.

Mostly she exists in the midst of an incredible interweaving of noise and music that flows through my life. I am referring to music as a metaphor for the realm of Divine presence, and to noise as a metaphor for the realm of Divine absence, or to be precise, the place where we are not in touch with the *experience* of God's presence. For a long time, I moved between the spiritual poles of presence and absence.

To play with the metaphor a bit more, we are apt to begin the contemplative journey by seeking out spaces where Divine music is more readily accessible and, avoiding the world of noise, which we think of as the mere influx of meaningless material. Eventually, though, we face a significant question: Can we perceive God in the raucous noise of living, just as we perceive God in the beautiful music of interior spiritual experience? Can we meet God in dog-barking and traffic horns and whining children and the infernal drone of the television?

Let me tell you a story. It is one of my earliest memories.

When I was four, a sound slipped into my bedroom and woke me up. It was a persistent sound of scratching on my window screen. It was an awful sound, really. Loud and grating, and given the darkness and shadowy images moving across the curtains, I suppose I could have become afraid. But I wasn't. I was struck only with curiosity, with a kind of wonder about this noise in the darkness. I remember lying in bed imagining increasingly magical explanations for it, unaware that I was about to engage a mystery that would in some way linger with me the rest of my life.

Armed with an array of vivid possibilities, I crept out of bed and made my way through the house to my parents' bed. I shook my mother's shoulder. "Mama, there is an angel scratching against my window."

I waited to hear what she would say. My mother did not say, "Don't be silly. That violates the rational abstraction of the traditional worldview!" She did not say, "The scratching on your window is only the wind dragging an old branch across the screen. It's nothing. Go back to bed."

Instead, even groggy with sleep, she knew that the ability to let go and listen creatively to the world as a mythic and sacred place, that the power to listen to the humdrum and the familiar and hear the sacred possibility of music inside it is a tender, fragile thing, easily lost. So rather than douse my first foray into holy imaginings, she put her blessing on it. She said, "An angel? Wonderful. Say hello for me."

That small, whimsical fragment of my childhood was the beginning of an awareness that has shaped much of my life since: Common noises are not always what they appear to be. They can also be the eloquence of God. It is all in the richness of listening. If we develop our deeper metaphysical ears, we may hear the music of divinity in uncommon places.

I've known a great deal of noise in my life, but I have also spent much time trying to tune my inner ear—the cochlea of my soul—to hear the Divine in the thick of my days, in the quarrel with my husband, the conversation with my teenage son, my daughter's shrill-giggling slumber parties, the death of my beloved spaniel, the wilting geranium in my kitchen— these scratchings upon my window.

There is an integration in the contemplative journey when dualities collapse, when the noise and the music become one sound.

∽

THE YOUNG MAN HAD LOST his job and didn't know which way to turn. He went to see an old preacher and paced about the preacher's study, ranting about his problem. Clenching his fist, he shouted, "I've begged God to say something to help me. Tell me, preacher, why doesn't God answer?"

The old preacher, who sat across the room, spoke some- thing in reply—something so hushed it was indistinguish- able. The young man stepped across the room. "What did you say?" he asked.

The preacher repeated himself, but again in a tone as

soft, barely audible. So the young man moved closer until he was leaning on the preacher's chair. "Sorry," he said. "I still didn't hear you."

When their heads bent together the old preacher spoke once more. "God sometimes speaks in whispers, so we will move closer to hear."

This time the young man heard.

⮀

SITTING ON THE CAROLINA SHORE, I cupped a small conch to my ear. Listening for the sound buried inside, I heard a faint, haunting echo that sounded like the whispering voice of the ocean.

There is a Scripture reference to the "still, small voice" of God—a lovely term that suggests the spark of God within. It is heard the same way as the sound in the conch shell. By cupping my ear to the ground of Being.

⮀

ONE EVENING AS I SAT in the rocker, working on a piece of needlepoint, I got one of those feelings of being watched.

Looking up, I saw my five-year-old son staring at me from the doorway. He wandered over and crawled into my lap.

"What do you want?" I asked.

"Nothing," he said. "I just want to be with you."

He laid his head on my arm, content to be near me, to curl up in my circle of lamplight and be in my presence.

The most beautiful prayer is to sit with God that way. To pray, not because I want something, not because I'm in trouble again, but because I simply want to be close.

ᕰ

As I sat in my den with the television droning in the background, I read about an autistic child who could not speak. She communicated within her silent world by writing on her computer screen. When a network news correspondent came to interview her and asked her what it was like to live with such silence, she wrote, "I hear God's finest whispers."

Surprised, the correspondent responded. "And what does God say?"

The girl typed on her keyboard, "He says he loves me too."

❧

THERE IS AN EXTRAORDINARY NEED in our lives for silence. The constant noise and chatter, internal and external, causes us to lose touch with the center of our being. When that happens, we become caught in all kinds of unimportant things. We suffer from this noise. Many of us even cling to this pollution of noise because it drowns out painful hungers inside. There is an old contemplative saying: "If you cannot improve the silence, do not speak."

STANDING FAST

I'VE OFTEN WONDERED at the gift some people have for enduring, whether enduring in the face of calamity or enduring in their beliefs when the entire world seems arranged against them.

Rosa Parks, Moses, Saint Teresa, Etty Hillesum, Julian of Norwich, Martin Luther, Dr. Martin Luther King, Jr., Gandhi, Sojourner Truth, Archbishop Desmond Tutu—they seem to possess the secret of winter foliage, a secret that keeps certain leaves steadfast in the bitterest season. They were, I suspect, distilled down again and again to the undying ground of God that underlies all being. Enduring comes from arriving at our own earned truth, knowing it inside, not because someone else tells us it is so or because we read it in a fine book, but because we have experienced it ourselves.

GROWING UP, I OFTEN HEARD my father say that "a person must stand on his scruples." I assumed scruples were principles, seeing as how being scrupulous meant being concerned with what is honest and right. But actually *scruple* means "a small, sharp stone." I read that the phrase "to stand on your scruples" derived from the idea of being bothered by a small, sharp stone in one's shoe, but standing there anyway. In other words, standing on your scruples is standing firm, but doing so with tender feet. With sensitivity.

Jesus seemed to teach a path of being lovingly principled, to have our scruples but stand fast with tender skin. If we grow a callous over our sensitivity, we may stand fast, but what a grim and inflexible standing that will be. There have been times when I've stood fast about something, but I was persevering out of a stubborn need to be right. It was principle for principle's sake, a heady ride with power. I was on my high horse and I needed to get off.

In the movie *Gandhi*, there's a scene in which Gandhi's

wife refuses to rake and cover the latrine in the new community that they have built, a community established on the principle that everyone must share the work equally. She asks Gandhi why he wants her, his wife, to do the work of untouchables. "It's not me, it's the principle," he tells her. When still she refuses, he grows angry and implacable, pushing her out the door, shouting, "Go then, leave this place!" Enslaved by the rightness of his principle, he loses sight of what matters—his wife, the woman before him with all her faults and complexities.

But then in a moment that never fails to touch me with its grace, he sees that his principle has become detached from the ground of love. The hardheartedness drains out of him. He undergoes a distillation right before our eyes. "What's wrong with me?" he asks. "I apologize." His transformation becomes the seed of her transformation. "I must go now," she tells him, "and rake and cover the latrine."

After this experience, Gandhi stands on his principles with unwavering dignity, yet never loses his compassion. People who are able to hold the balance between love and principle are those who carry the humbling awareness that they are capable of breaking every principle they hold, of abandoning each truth they espouse, of caving in a thousand times. This keeps them human; it keeps them real. It saves them from becoming arrogant and intractable in their righteousness.

We must stand with grit—yes, of course. But we must do so with tenderness for the smallest thing.

∽

I HAD COME TO A DELICATE PLACE in my life when I needed to find the courage to be myself.

Walking around the lake at Kanuga Conference Center, I pondered my need to voice my own truths and explore my own path even when it deviated from expectations around me.

Finally, I sat on a bench and gazed across the water at a small flotilla of ducks paddling in unison. When one duck turned, they all turned. When one quacked, they all quacked. They even speeded up and slowed down at the same time. As I watched them zigzag along predictably, I noticed one single duck swimming with the others, but clearly cutting her own path through the water. She sometimes turned left when they turned right, took little adventures on her own, and quacked when the others were quiet.

I laughed out loud. She was clearly her own duck! She made me bolder.

⟡

IT WAS THE LAST ROUND of the Masters golf tournament. I stood pressed in the crowd around the fifteenth green. Suddenly a thousand heads turned in the same direction. Jack Nicklaus was striding down the fairway. "When God handed out golf talent, that man got an extra helping," said a man behind me.

Nicklaus was only a few shots off the lead and was making a charge. This hole was crucial. Out in the fairway, he planted his feet over the ball. There was only one way to the green— over a pond of water. Nicklaus swung. The ball soared up, then blip! It disappeared into the water, near the edge.

The gallery groaned. Nicklaus marched over and looked down where the little white ball was stuck in the mud under half a foot of water. He took off his shoes and his socks, rolled up his trousers, and waded into the pond. He was refusing to give up a penalty shot. He was going to try to hit the ball out of the water! With the crowd completely hushed, Nicklaus slashed his club into the water. For a second he disappeared in the spray, and then I saw it—the ball hurtling straight for the pin. It landed close to the hole. Nicklaus made a birdie.

Afterward, I wondered if it was his extra helping of talent that did it. Maybe. But it seemed to me that what I'd seen was more about sheer determination than anything else.

We each have our own share of talent, but what makes the difference is boldness. Grit. Determination.

∽

I HEAD A STORY about a promising art student whose finished painting was so impressive that his teacher not only exclaimed over it, but called the other students so that they could see how he put the lessons to brilliant use.

That night a hot water pipe burst in the classroom and turned the painting into a mess of bleeding colors.

"It's ruined," the student said.

"No, not at all," said the teacher. "The real work was what you learned in your mind. Now use it to create an even better painting."

I think of all the times we've been told to put our failures behind us. Perhaps we should leave our successes behind too.

∾

DURING THOSE TIMES when I wonder what I'm going to do with my life and I'm unable to envision it, I recall a dot-to-dot picture of a giraffe—a gift from a four-year-old. The child had created the picture by moving his pencil from dot to dot, one at a time. It comforts me to know that when I can't see the whole picture, all I really need is to see the next dot.

∾

WALKING ALONE on Horseshoe Beach in Bermuda where great rocks dot the shoreline, I came upon an unusual boulder towering at the water's edge. There was a hole through the center, so large that the rock resembled a hoop. *How peculiar,* I thought. *However did it get that way?*

As I watched the water splash against the rock—wave after wave, spilling through the opening—I realized that it was not the water but the persistence of the sea that had made a way through the impossible. Walking on, I thought how easily I had sometimes given up on problems or dreams that had seemed too hard, too impenetrable.

Persistent love. Persistent hope. Persistent effort. The mystery of overcoming often lay in the simple rhythmic act of keeping at it.

∾

RABBI JOSEPH LIEBERMANN told how he fell asleep one night and had a dream. In the dream he dies and goes to stand before the judgment seat of God. As he waits for God to speak, he fears that the Lord will ask him, "Why weren't you a Moses . . . or a David . . . or a Solomon?" But God surprises him. He simply asks, "Why weren't you Rabbi Liebermann?"

When my life is over, I doubt God will ask me why I wasn't a Mother Teresa. The question I fear most is, "Why weren't you Sue Monk Kidd?"

The most gracious and courageous gift we can offer the world is our authenticity, our uniqueness, the expression of our true selves.

⟡

As I WALKED TO THE MAILBOX that Monday, the clouds were the color of nickel, round and silver and rumbling just a little, like the rattle of a piggy bank. I glanced at the sky as two or three drops of rain splashed on me. I was not surprised. It seemed like it had been raining on me since I got out of bed.

The storm had started when my thirteen-year-old son, Bob, and I had argued earlier that morning. He'd wanted to wear an old, faded sweatshirt with cutoff sleeves to school, and I insisted on the nice, new shirt his grandmother had given him for Christmas, the kind with the button-down collar and blue monogram on the pocket. I'd pointed to the letters. "It's not everybody that has his initials on his shirt," I said reasonably.

He had rolled his eyes to the kitchen ceiling. "Nobody wears initials on their shirts, Mama. Nobody!"

Soon we were shouting. He said awful things. I said awful things. Finally he'd yanked on the grandmother-shirt. As he picked up his books, I'd reached over to give him a hug, but he stiffened and drew back.

The truth was, I wasn't sure how to deal with Bob since he'd entered the world of adolescence. He'd scarcely arrived in it, and already we were skidding into little puddles of rebellion that left me feeling exasperated. He was a fine boy, a good son, but there were days he questioned everything I said. Days he seemed to test me deliberately. There'd been so much conflict and quarreling between us lately I was ready to throw up my hands and quit.

Shaking away the morning's events, I sighed and walked on toward the mailbox, which looked as defeated as I felt. Ever since a car had plowed into the side of it, the pole had been bent and the door hung ajar.

Reaching inside, my hand brushed against a stack of envelopes—then something peculiar, like broom bristles. I peered inside. The day's mail sat on top of a small collection of weeds and pine straw. Somebody's idea of a prank, I decided.

As I raked it out, a drop of rain splatted on my face. I shuffled toward the house, not bothering to hurry.

That afternoon Bob breezed in from school and disappeared into his room. "How was your day?" I said, tagging behind him, trying to ignore the rift between us.

"Okay," he said, pulling off his shirt. He tossed the monogrammed thing on the floor at my feet. I glared at it, like he'd thrown down a gauntlet. He rummaged through his drawer for the inevitable cutoff sweatshirt. I wheeled around to leave, then turned back. "Did you put pine straw in the mailbox?" I asked.

He gave me a confused look. "What?"

"Never mind," I said.

The next day when I went to the mailbox, it was there again. A smattering of pine straw, some twigs, two dead dandelions.

Each day I found a bouquet of weeds in the mailbox. And each day I whisked it out. I didn't bring up the subject with Bob again. As a matter of fact, I quit discussing anything with Bob. Every time a conflict arose, I simply flexed my authority, then left the room or changed the subject. It was just easier that way.

On Saturday Bob wandered into the den where I was reading the newspaper. "Mama, can I go to the movies?" he asked. I flipped the newspaper to the theater section. The movie he was asking about was rated PG-13. The number thirteen indicated an extra note of caution to parents. I looked at my *thirteen*-year-old son. The irony was not lost on me.

"Nope, not this movie," I answered.

"Can't we even talk about it?" he pleaded.

"There's nothing to talk about," I said. "We would only end up shouting again."

"Mama, you don't understand," he cried. "You don't even try!"

When mail time came again, I walked out as usual and there was the same maddening bundle of debris. Reaching in to pull it out, I caught a flash of something small, round, and blue in the twigs and straw. It was a bird's egg.

Chirping burst from a nearby tree. Scanning the limbs, I spotted the mother bird with a piece of pine straw dangling from her beak. I pushed the ragged nest back inside, impressed by her tenacity. Every day she had started a nest inside our broken mailbox and when she returned to find her efforts whisked away, she had tried again.

"You don't even try!" Bob had said to me.

He sat beside his desk absently turning his globe around. "Hi," I said. He looked up at me and stared, and for an instant I glimpsed the vulnerable little boy he'd once been, as well as the young man he was becoming. "Wanna talk?" I asked. "I promise to listen."

My sitting there, listening to him pour out his anger and resentment and needs seemed to soak up the pain between us and give us a new beginning.

Later we printed a sign: "Dear Mailman, A bird has built her nest inside the mailbox. Would you deliver our mail to the front door until her eggs hatch and the birds fly away?"

Three baby birds appeared in our mailbox. Every day the mother perched on top of it and sang. It was the song that would get me through the teenage years—the sweet, stubborn sound of love that never quits.

LETTING GO

AS A GIRL, playing along the mushy banks of my grand-father's pond, I found a small green turtle and took it home. My mother let me have an old Dutch kettle, which I turned into a turtle house. I placed water, sand, grass and several dead flies inside the kettle, thinking any turtle would be thrilled to live there. The turtle, however, spent every waking minute going in circles trying to climb up the side and escape. After a week, though, it stopped and just sat there.

"It never moves anymore," I told my grandfather.

"It misses being a real turtle," he said. "That's all."

The two of us carried it back to the pond, where I let it go, a little tearfully as I recall. As the turtle scurried blissfully away, Granddaddy said, "The best thing you ever do for those you love is set them free."

Now when I'm tempted to start building turtle houses for other people to live in, imposing my own ideas and visions on them, I try to recall this memory and set them free to be themselves.

✑

I WATCHED FROM THE WINDOW as my five-year-old son galloped across the grass on an imaginary horse. His head bobbed under a heap of Indian feathers, looking as if a giant peacock had landed in his hair. He clutched a brand new bow in one hand and a rubber-tipped arrow in the other.

Reining his horse to a stop under the maple trees, he placed the arrow into his bow and took aim at the sky. The arrow took a limp nosedive to the ground a few inches in front of him. He tried several times, but the arrow refused to take off.

"My arrow won't shoot," he told me, dragging his bow behind him into the house.

I smiled at him under all those drooping feathers and shook my head. "I know. You didn't draw back enough." Archery had been one of my favorite pastimes when I was a child. My father had set up a bull's-eye in the backyard, and I'd spent hours out there learning how to pull back the arrow and hold it steady for several seconds before releasing it. The secret was in that moment of taut repose.

I gave Bob a quick demonstration, then he went back outside and sent an arrow onto our neighbor's roof. The power of withdrawing at the right moment is one of the easiest things to forget. That instant of pulling back into focused stillness.

∽

I HAD FOUND LITTLE RELIEF from the burden I was carrying around. Someone I loved was ill, and I could actually feel a heaviness inside from the weight of it.

One night, anxious to sleep, I slipped into my daughter's room to make sure she was covered. The night-light glowed through the organdy ruffle of her canopied bed, and as I suspected, her blanket had been kicked off. Tucking the cover over her, I noticed that she clutched a half-eaten grape lollipop in her hand, a birthday present from her grandmother. She had carried it around all day. Now it had made a sticky purple splotch on the pillowcase, and a few strands of her hair were stuck to it.

Oh, for Pete's sake, why didn't she get rid of this before going to bed? I pried her fingers from the candy, wondering if the reason I had found so little peace was because I'd been praying with my fingers wrapped tightly around my need, unwilling to trust anything so precious out of my sight.

Holding her purple lollipop, I kissed my daughter's face and let go. Her lollipop, my burden—they were in good hands.

～

WARM SUN, SOFT BREEZE, HAZY SKY—it's that kind of day on the Carolina coast. We bounce along in a chartered tour boat, speeding through dark green backwater on our way around the peninsula. A salty wind blows across the deck, disappearing into the roar of the engine.

Soon we are climbing waves, sliding over bulges, the marshes behind us. Then the engines are cut off, the drone dies away. We rock on the surface. The captain points to a jetty. I lift binoculars to my eyes. On the rocks, congregating like a chorus line waiting in the wings, are *hundreds* of pelicans.

Bags of popcorn are passed through the crowd on board. One by one we empty them over the sides until the kernels bob across the water. Feeding the birds is part of the tour.

Suddenly the air explodes with a whirling profusion of feathers. Pelicans fill the sky. They spin around the boat like a carousel, scooping popcorn from the sea. I even wonder for a moment if perhaps they are not doing this for the food at all, but for the sheer joy of flying over our boat.

All the children on board begin to skip around the deck, reaching their arms to the birds. It is an irresistible urge. I, too, feel the moment.

The pelicans sweep up and down the sky like jubilant chords of music. My children skip by. One of them reaches out a hand. And I grab on. I am skipping, too.

❦

I WAITED OUTSIDE THE SCHOOL to pick up my third-grade-son. A yellow bus filled the school driveway. A crossing guard led a parade of children across an intersection. Above, an Indian summer sun tinted the world red and gold.

I watched Bob amble along the sidewalk with an over-sized book satchel on his back.

"Hi," I said, as he climbed into the front seat of the car.

He grinned at me and waved at a friend pedaling by on a bicycle. "Mama, can I ride my bike to school?" he asked.

I didn't answer immediately. Instead my mind tumbled back to his first day of school. It had been hard to let him go—so small and untouched—into the risks and hurts of the world. It had seemed he was stepping over an invisible line and nothing would ever be the same again. He'd walked into his classroom slowly, then turned and waved. I'd watched, feeling something tear inside me.

Now those same unsettling echoes of finality rippled through me again. A seven-year-old going to school and back on his own. Pedaling by himself. Without me. "I don't think so," I replied.

"But it's not far."

"No."

"I'll be eight soon." His face was crunched up with long-ing, so much that I had to look away.

"Not yet," I said quietly.

He started to argue again, but thought better of it. We drove home in silence.

Each day it was the same tug-of-war. "Mama, what about today? Can I ride my bike today?"

We pulled the little piece of freedom back and forth. Probably it was silly. The trip was five blocks in a safe, small-town neighborhood. But I couldn't seem to help it. Surely I wasn't wrong to be so protective, I told myself.

"I'm not a baby anymore," he explained to me one Friday night as I told him good night.

"No, I suppose not."

Saturday dawned the perfect autumn day, bright and cool with a breezy wind that had blown the clouds high.

I took the children to the mall. As we walked along, peering in store windows, we noticed a man with a cluster of helium-filled balloons. We bought two. One blue. One yellow. The man placed the strings in Bob's and Ann's hands, and the children strolled away, pulling the balloons casually through the air.

"Watch out," I said, pointing up to where half a dozen escaped balloons hung from the ceiling. That was all it took.

They wound the strings around their wrists with nervous glances upward.

As we emerged from JCPenney into the gilded afternoon, sure enough, the inevitable happened. Bob stumbled on the curb, and as he reached out to catch himself, the string slipped away. His balloon sailed over the parking lot, the little string waving behind it. He stood there and gaped at it with disappointment. I braced for his protests. But as the balloon floated higher and higher, climbing to an astonishing height, his face changed from sadness to surprise, even pride. "Wow! Look how far mine is going!" he cried.

It really was a spectacle. Lots more thrilling than the sight of it bobbing just above his head. Standing beside her brother, still clutching her yellow balloon, Ann spontaneously opened her palm and let it go. It swept up to the sky, chasing after the other one. We pointed at them, laughing and exclaiming till they were nearly out of sight.

Back home, as I pulled into the carport, the first thing I spotted was Bob's bicycle leaning against the bricks. It was plain to me—I was holding on too tightly, keeping Bob from the horizons in his world. My son was a balloon tied to my wrist. If I kept him there, he would be safe and sheltered, but he would not go very far.

On Monday, once again the sky was inordinately bright and blue, not a hint of the rain I almost wished would come and postpone this moment. Bob climbed on his bicycle, trying to look grown up, to suppress his eagerness. I took a deep breath. "Okay, God, he's in your hands."

It was a small thing, letting him make his own way to school, so small, one might wonder why I would even chronicle it. My answer is because sometimes you can glimpse the essence of something in a tiny fragment of it—like seeing the oak in the acorn or the ocean in a wave. So much of parenthood is negotiating endings, the unceasing process of disconnecting the strings that tie our children to us, preparing them for a life on their own. That has always been the ache and beauty of it for me—taking the deep breath and trusting somehow in the goodness of life, in God, in something beyond myself.

At the edge of the driveway Bob stopped and looked back at me over his shoulder.

"Mama?"

"What?"

"Don't worry, I'll be fine. Okay?"

"Okay."

I watched him pedal down the street. Then he was gone, disappearing into the morning.

~

BOXES ARE STREWN across the floor of my son's room in various stages of packing. Two tan suitcases lie open on the bed. The drawers in his dresser jut out like stair steps, almost empty. I stand in the doorway and watch Bob sort through the items in his room, deciding which ones he'll take to college and which ones he'll leave behind.

I can hardly comprehend this moment. *Dear God,* I think, *I give birth to a baby and feed him carrots; I swoon when he says ma-ma and rock him all night when he gets a fever. I sing him silly songs and read him books and teach him to ride a bike and beam when he catches a fly ball in Little League. And now I stand in the doorway, bewildered as he packs up to leave.*

I watch Bob pick up a book he got as a graduation gift. It's titled *Oh, the Places You'll Go!* and has a swirling rainbow on the cover. He ponders it a moment. "Dr. Seuss?" he says a little indignantly. "It's a children's book!"

That had been my sentiment, too, until I read the book jacket: "The perfect send-off for children starting out in the maze of life, be they nursery school grads or medical school achievers."

But Bob sets the book back on the shelf, unimpressed.

There was a time, of course, when my son would have done somersaults at receiving a Dr. Seuss book. Somewhere in the garage there's a box of them, along with all the other discarded remnants of his childhood.

I let out a sigh, wondering how this moment of life has arrived so quickly. Yesterday my child was sitting on my lap reading *The Cat in the Hat*. Tomorrow he is going to college. I wonder if he's ready to be on his own. I wonder if *I'm* ready for him to be on his own. Sending a child off into the world is a new thing for me and I don't like the way it makes me feel.

Across the room Bob pulls his baseball glove from the

closet. "I may need this," he tells me, dropping it in a box. "The university has intramurals."

"That sounds like fun," I say.

"Mama, do you know where my baseball cleats are?"

"I'll look in the garage." I hurry off, glad to escape the sight of his room being stripped bare.

The garage is layered with all the stuff we can't bring ourselves to throw out. We're a dozen garage sales behind. I look in several places for the cleats, without luck. Finally, I rummage through a box in the corner. At the bottom of it is the minnow net that I bought four-year-old Bob when Sandy and I took him for a summer vacation at the beach. I sink down onto the cool cement floor and stare at it through a blur of tears.

That vacation Bob and I concocted a daily ritual. We would go to the beach first thing every morning, spread out our towel and read Dr. Seuss's *One Fish Two Fish Red Fish Blue Fish*. When we finished, I would say, "Ready to catch red fish and blue fish?" And Bob would take off with his new minnow net, skimming for fish, while I'd tag behind him.

Fourteen years later I can see it clearly: the chrome-colored waves sliding in and out. Bob, small and tawny-skinned, with this little net flung over his shoulder.

I have not cried yet over this nest-emptying experience, but now my grief spills out. Grief for the little boy chasing blue fish. I'm surprised it hurts this much.

Later that night I wander back into Bob's room. "Did you ever read that Dr. Seuss book you got for graduation?" I ask. He shakes his head.

"Me either," I say. I pull it off the shelf, plop down on the bed and open it.

I scan a few pages. It's filled with inimitable Seuss rhymes and illustrations. "Listen to this," I say to Bob, who's playing a video game across the room.

He protests. "*Aw*, Mama."

But I read out loud anyway:

"Today is your day.

You're off to Great Places!

You're off and away! . . .

Oh, the places you'll go!"

The rhymes are about a young fellow setting out into life

with all its ups and downs, traveling to amazing places and experiencing amazing things, all on his own. Bob flicks off the video game and peers over my shoulder at a picture of this fellow meeting up with several menacing gremlins that look a lot like frankfurters with green eyes.

As I read, Bob chuckles. Sometimes I chuckle too. The heaviness I've been feeling fades.

One of the last pictures shows the dauntless adventurer single-handedly pulling a mountain behind him like a wagon.

When I close the book, I notice Bob's eyes are fired with eager anticipation.

That night I do not sleep. I keep thinking about tomorrow. I keep trying to get the minnow net out of my dreams.

The next afternoon Bob, his father and I drive to the campus, winding through red-brick, white-columned buildings and sprawling southern oaks. It's a nice place. Big, but nice.

It takes six trips from the car, up three flights to Bob's dormitory room in order to haul all the stuff he's brought. I help him stack his clothes in the drawer. "Remember, wash the whites separate from the darks. And don't wash wool. It shrinks," I tell him.

"I know, Mama," he says. I look at him. Does he? Does he really know all these things? There are suddenly about fifty other pieces of motherly advice I want to bestow on him. I have a particular urge to mention that he should not go around in short sleeves in thirty-degree weather, or skip breakfast, or wait till the last minute to write his term papers, three things he's bad about doing. But I keep quiet. These are gremlins he's going to have to face on his own.

I arrange a blue rug across the tile floor of his dorm room, then tuck a blanket over his bed. His father helps him nail a poster on the wall. Too quickly, it's all done. We walk down the steps in silence. We pause on the sidewalk beside the car and stand, looking awkwardly at one another, trying to figure out how to say good-bye.

He's wearing his all-star baseball cap, grinning at us from under the bill. His daddy grabs him and gives him a hug. Then Bob turns to me. I reach for him and hold him. Then I turn loose. It is nearly the hardest thing I've ever done in my life. "You'll be fine," I tell him. Sandy and I stand on the sidewalk and watch him walk away. At the corner of the dormitory he looks back and waves.

That night I go to the garage and take the minnow net from the box. I carry it into Bob's room, where I hang it on the wall beside his high school senior picture. In the lamplight the picture takes on a golden reflection, and the net seems to shine from the rays of a sunlit beach. I stare at both a long while, pondering the seasons of love in a mother's life, knowing there's a time to hold and a time to let go, a time to tag along and a time to wave good-bye.

Then I turn to the window, my heart traveling far into the night. "Oh, Son, the places you'll go!" I whisper.

I WAS TALKING WITH a young woman named Kathy, who had just completed a rock climbing course. "The hardest part was the blindfolded climb," she told me. "I was up on the rock face unable to see a thing, not knowing which direction to move. A guide below was calling directions to me like, 'Move your hand a few inches to the left and you'll find a crevice.' In the beginning I was so afraid I couldn't focus on what he was saying. It finally hit me that the only way I was going to make it down was to concentrate on his voice and follow his directions, step by step."

When I come upon one of those places where I can't see which way to turn next, my best response has been like hers: to quiet my anxiety and focus on the voice of the guide within myself. There is a source of divine wisdom in us that simply knows. A nudge, an awareness, a dream, an intuitive flash, a gradual dawning, a gut reaction—guidance comes from within, step by tiny step.

∾

WHEN MY DAUGHTER ANN entered her teens, we went through an adjustment period. One morning she came out of her room wearing an odd combination of clothes. "You're not going to school like *that*, are you?" I asked.

She planted her feet. "I was planning on it!" Our voices rose. Before she left, we were both in tears.

Later a friend asked me, "Was it really her choice of clothes that was bothering you?"

Sure it was, I thought. But the question needled me. I sat in Ann's room and tried to figure it out. As I stared at her closet, I remembered how I used to dress her myself, wrestling her ponytail through turtleneck sweaters matching her ribbons to her skirts. I bit my bottom lip. What was *really* bothering me was that she was growing up.

"Be patient with me," I told Ann that evening. "It's hard letting go."

"I know, Mama," she said. "It's hard for me too. Sometimes I wish I was still small enough for you to dress."

⌒

ON MOVING DAY, as my husband Sandy puts the last box on the truck, I stand in the bedroom trying to figure out how to say good-bye to the home my family has lived in for the last fifteen years. This has been our first house, the place our children have grown up, where our lives have been woven together with moments good and bad. Now it is empty.

Beyond the window I see the maple tree Bob climbed as a boy. "Look, Mama, look how high I am!" His voice is still out there floating in the branches. At the base of the tree is the spot where Ann buried her time capsule, preserving for future generations her first-grade drawings and a picture of herself in a ballerina costume. How does a person leave such things? For the first time, I feel the sadness of moving, the particular heaviness that intrudes into the heart when it's time to walk away from something loved.

The move has come about in a rather mysterious way. On a Sunday afternoon several weeks earlier, a real estate agent knocked on our door. "I have a couple who would like to see your house," she said.

Sandy and I exchanged baffled glances. "But our house isn't for sale!" we cried practically in unison.

"I know, but it's just the sort of house this couple is looking for."

This made no sense. Everywhere there were houses for sale. The economy was in a recession, the housing industry mired in a slump.

The agent must have read our disbelieving faces. "I know this must seem unusual to you," she went on. "But you see, I saw your house a couple of years ago when it was on the market, and when this couple described what they wanted, your house popped into my mind."

Two years ago we had indeed put our house up for sale in hopes of finding one with space for me to have a study. But after a few weeks, a feeling of reluctance came over me—not the sadness of leaving, but a feeling that it wasn't the right time to move. One day while a family viewed the house, the nudge grew so strong that I had found myself telling them the shrubbery was dying and sometimes when it rained water stood under the house for weeks. Sandy had stared at me aghast. "I see why you're not in sales," he had commented after they left.

The next morning we had called our real estate agent and asked him to take down the For Sale sign.

Then two years later this agent appeared on our doorstep. Was it time to think again about moving?

That night I had a dream: I was walking toward a house I'd never seen before. It was a two-story, white house with a bright red roof.

We decided to proceed with the idea of moving and see what happened. We invited the interested couple to see our home. Things fell into place with almost dazzling speed. They made a nice offer and we contacted a realtor to help us look over the market.

Driving to the first house, I was skeptical, but a few minutes later the realtor stopped at a white two-story house with a red roof. I leaned over to Sandy. "I think we're going to live here."

After a tour inside, we both agreed. Within a week we had sold our house and bought the new one.

But now, on moving day, despite the uncanny sense of guidance I felt, despite my excitement over the new house, it is painful to leave the familiar warmth of this place we've lived in for so many years.

I walk from one room to another, saying farewell. To the floorboard that creaked beneath the rocking chair; to the dear marks marching up the back of the closet door, measuring the children's heights; to the spot by the fireplace where Sandy and I spent so many winter evenings watching the flames.

When Sandy comes back inside, I am staring into the fireplace at a half-burned log on a mound of ashes, the remains of the last fire burned the winter before.

"Okay," he says, "we're packed and ready to go."

Ready? I gaze at the hearth, shaking my head.

His eyes follow my gaze to the hearth. "Oh right. We forgot to clean out the fireplace," he says, missing my point. He traipses out to the truck and returns with a broom, dustpan, and an extra moving carton. He opens the glass screen, places the charred log into the box, then sweeps up the ashes.

"Would you dump the ashes out back?" he says, handing me the dustpan. While he loads the box with the log inside it onto the moving truck, I wander into the backyard and toss the ashes into the trash, then climb into the truck. At the end of the street, Sandy reaches over and wipes the tears sliding off my cheeks.

Over the next several weeks I unpack, trying to adjust to our new surroundings, lovely but unfamiliar. Nothing seems like home. As ridiculous as it seems I miss the old house.

One day while out shopping I drive by it. The maple tree has turned red. It is ablaze with sunlight, every leaf aflame. It brings a severe pang of homesickness. I sigh. I am still trying to say good-bye!

That evening a cold front presses down from the North

Carolina mountains. Sitting in the den of our new house, I feel the cold lapping around the doors. "*B-r-r-r,*" I say.

Sandy puts down his magazine and leaves the room. He reappears with a box, a moving carton. I groan. "I thought we'd unpacked all those."

"I've been saving this one in the garage." He smiles. "Open it."

I peel back the lid. Beneath the rustle of newspaper is a sooty, half-burned log.

A smoky scent drifts up. "You saved the log from our old house!"

"For the first fire in our new one," he says.

As he lays the log in the fireplace, I add some kindling and strike a match. The old log ignites, leaping to flame, an incandescent bridge between old and new. We sit before it on the carpet, not speaking, staring at the tendrils of fire.

I think about the unceasing migrations of the human heart. How we move not only from house to house, but from one phase of life to another, from relationship to relationship, career to career, awareness to awareness. The saving grace in these moments is our willingness to leave the old—taking the cherished lessons and experiences with us and embracing the new with acceptance and grace.

The log crackled, sending a spiral of red sparks up the flue of winter. For the first time, it felt like home.

∾

HIGH IN THE MOUNTAINS of North Carolina snow was falling on the roof of the cabin where my husband Sandy and I were spending New Year's Eve. We sat beside the fireplace, watching the flames. As midnight drew near, we talked about the year just past—the joys we'd had but also our sadnesses and regrets.

"Wouldn't it be nice to burn all the failures of the past year and start clean?" Sandy said. It was, I think, a rhetorical question, but I went scrounging around for pencils and paper.

We wrote down the things we didn't want to carry with us into the new year. I filled up one side of the page and started on the other.

At the stroke of midnight we let our lists float down into the fire and watched the edges of the paper curl, then ignite.

The next day I raked the gray ashes from the fireplace and dumped them behind the cabin just as a gust of wind rose. The old year went swirling into the clean, white morning. It was a new beginning.

REBORN TO LOVE

ONCE WHILE SPEAKING to a group of women, I said
that God can be experienced in the act of lovemaking in profound and beautiful ways, just as God can be
experienced in the act of meditation. I noticed that a
woman in the second row literally covered her ears with her
hands. She came up to me afterward and said, "I don't think
you should mix those two things." Having an uncontrol-
lable impish streak at times, I said, "What two things?" And
she said, "You know, God and lovemaking." For her, lovemaking was a place devoid of divine music. She did not like
mixing what she had neatly divided into sacred and profane,
spirit and matter.

Yet sexuality is also a sacrament. For a woman especially,
Eros is experienced as Divine. Lovemaking brings her into

the holy experience of *hieros gamos*, the sacred marriage of her deep feminine and creative masculine. It brings her to the numinous and unitive experience with the Other.

The spiritual life is an expanding awareness of the Divine as all in all, vividly and actually present in all external reality, without dualistic separations. Here is the simple truth I keep trying to own, the one that breaks the bounds of beauty: everything is in God and God is in everything.

⟨∾

BEING AN EXCESSIVELY ignorant gardener, I planted two pines, a magnolia, a spruce and three cedars in my backyard in the middle of winter. They were tiny, not one over eighteen inches.

My gardener friends shook their heads. "You can't transplant trees now," they all exclaimed. Not one of them believed the trees would survive.

But I loved those trees and I decided I would do whatever I could to save them, even if it was unconventional. I'd read about an experiment that reported that talking to plants enhanced their growth. I know. It sounds completely foolish. But this was a scientific experiment.

I began to go outside (when my neighbors weren't around) and say a few kind words to my trees—that I cared about their growth and believed they would flourish. While I was out there, I also watered them, pulled up weeds and clipped away surrounding branches that blocked their sunlight.

Two years later, every one of those trees is stalwart and more than shoulder-high. They reflect a most beautiful truth: Never give up on what you love. Going against the odds and bestowing care and affirming words on a life that is struggling is the stuff of miracles. Whether a tree or a human being.

❧

"DADDY, BUILD ME A DOGHOUSE for Scruffy," begged our five-year-old daughter, Ann. She squeezed the brown puppy in her arms and gazed at my husband with that look I suppose no father can resist, because to my amazement he said, "Okay, we'll build a house for Scruffy."

"Will it have a roof and a door and his name on the front and everything?" she asked.

"It will have everything," he assured her.

For hours Sandy hammered and sawed a pile of new

lumber into something resembling a doghouse. When it was finished, it had a roof and a door and a name on the front and everything.

I smiled at his tired face. "You are probably the only father in the history of the world who had made a doghouse for a *stuffed* animal."

Surely the most endearing of love's attributes is its insistence on being impractical.

My husband and I were vacationing on the Carolina coast. He was on his beach towel. I was on mine. We'd been reading through the afternoon, hardly exchanging words except for an occasional, "Pass the suntan lotion." I looked up from my book, noticing our silhouettes on the sand, aware suddenly of the distance that had crept between us the last few months.

We'd been busy, preoccupied, going in different directions. The demands and details of everyday life—paying the mortgage, helping children with homework, getting the oil changed in the car—had nearly drowned out the intimacy between us.

The realization left me feeling a little melancholy.

That night I retreated to the screened porch of the beach cottage, "What's the matter?" Sandy asked, joining me. "You've been unusually quiet."

I hesitated, then blurted it out. "I was thinking about our marriage—how distant we've become lately. Sometimes it's like we're living in two separate worlds. I—I miss you."

"I miss you too," he said.

A few minutes later we were strolling arm in arm along the beach. "One day we ought to renew our wedding vows," I said.

"No time like the present," he responded.

I don't remember everything we said. Mostly I remember standing on the shore with the waves curling around our bare feet, hearing my husband say, "I promise to nurture the closeness between us." And I remember thinking that we had come home to what really matters in life.

ᥲᨆ

HE WAS EIGHTY when his first letter arrived at my house. He'd met me, he said, in the pages of *Guideposts*. For six years his letters came once a month without fail. Warm stories about his farm, the Scottish music he loved, the spinning wheels he made in his workshop, his love of poetry. Not once did he ever ask me to write back.

Sometimes little presents arrived mysteriously without a card. A honey drizzle, homemade wooden toys for the children, a worn book, an old album of Scottish music, framed poems written in a familiar shaky scrawl. I always knew exactly where the gifts had come from.

One May his letter didn't come. In June, I opened the mailbox to find his familiar handwriting on an envelope. "By the time you read this," Mr. Card wrote, "I shall have gone on to my next great adventure. This last letter is to thank you for letting me love you. . . ."

Today that letter—which he'd requested be mailed to me at his death—portrays the highest form of love: to ask not how much do you love me, but rather how much can I love *you*? To love without expectation.

∾

I HAVE ONE OF THOSE wooden Russian nesting dolls. If you open her up, you find another doll inside, and if you open that

one up, you find still another doll. In fact, you can keep opening until you have nine separate dolls standing in a row, each
one complete and individual, each able to stand on her own.
And yet, there is not a moment when I look at them unaware
that these dolls are part of the whole, that they all belong
together. They are separate, yes, but they are also inseparable.

I believe the human family, and indeed all creation, is
fashioned something like that nesting doll. Each part is
unique and independent, but nevertheless inextricably
linked, ever belonging to the larger whole. We contain the
other and are ourselves contained.

❧

DURING A PARTICULARLY painful time, I sat in my bedroom,
tears glazing my eyes. I'd offered my hurt to God, but the aching
hadn't stopped yet. Healing, I knew, took time, and tears were
part of the process. They made wet splotches on my blouse.

That's how my husband Sandy found me when he arrived
home from work. He didn't say a word, but in what is surely
one of the most precious moments of our marriage, he
touched his finger to the tears winding down my face, then

touched his wet finger to his own cheek. His gesture went straight to my heart, saying more than words ever could. Inexplicably, my sadness lightened, as if he had taken half of it into himself.

It is a profound gift to share another person's suffering, simply to be there, willing to blend your tears with theirs.

❧

WHEN MY DAUGHTER WAS SIX, she got her wish. A goldfish. She named him Spanky. Ann printed his name with a backward *S* on a slip of paper and taped it to his bowl. As an afterthought she drew a heart with an arrow through it beneath his name.

He would flash through the glass bowl on her dresser with what we came to think of as "personality." Ann would push her nose against the glass and watch for as long as a six-year-old can remain still while Spanky circled the transparent boundary of his world. She never seemed to tire of watching him swim and sometimes called me to observe how he "blew kisses" with his puckered mouth. The invisible strings between her heart and the fishbowl were so strong they sometimes tugged her in from play, inducing her to stand for a long, enthralled moment by his bowl before dashing back out.

One morning I found Ann by the fishbowl, unmoving.

Spanky lay on his side in the water. Small, golden, and obviously gone.

"Do fish sleep?" she asked.

Before I could answer, she ran to me and buried herself in my arms. "Oh, Mama!"

I held her tight. This was more than the death of a goldfish. It was the death of her friend. A good friend who had filled her moments with pleasure. Now she was crushed and I almost wished she had never loved him at all.

My eyes wandered to the slip of paper on which she'd printed his name, to the heart pierced with an arrow. She had unknowingly penciled the truth and fastened it to her fishbowl: Love always has its risky side, its painful side. There are no guarantees that the ones we love will live forever or that they will even return our love at all.

As Ann clung to me and cried, I thought how innocently I'd plunged into loving my grandfather when I was her age, and how much hurt had come when he'd died. I thought of how recklessly I'd once expressed my love to someone and had it shoved back at me. Every experience of love had the potential of being a heart shot through with an arrow. Even God had wounds from loving.

Ann looked at me and sniffed deeply. "Spanky was a good fish," she said, trying to keep her voice from trembling.

Shining in her eyes was the growth, strength, and beauty that comes from having loved with one's whole heart. I felt then what I'd always wanted to believe. Love is more joyful than the hurt is painful. It is always worth the risk of loving.

NO ONE KNEW EXACTLY who she was. The nurses called her Sunshine Lady. She always came sporadically and unexpectedly to the hospital's pediatric wing, leaving gifts for the children.

I remember one evening when I was the nurse on duty, she arrived with a big mysterious box.

Later, when I made rounds, I found a brand new teddy bear tucked beside every sick child.

Not one of the children would ever know who brought

the huggable companion to share their hospital experience. She got no tributes, no credit. Loving anonymously was enough.

∽

ALL DAY THE SUN HIBERNATED in the gray clouds. In its absence, a winter wind had woven the corners of the kitchen window with tiny patterns of ice. Four small frosty spider-webs. I stared at them, recalling the words my husband and I had exchanged before breakfast. It hadn't been a big argument. Just silly, angry words. But they'd hurt nonetheless. A stew simmered and I turned to give it a stir, replaying his last cutting remark before he'd left for work. Even now something ugly inside me wanted to retaliate . . . insult for insult.

My son plopped down on the kitchen floor with his "Magic Slate" while I paced about getting dinner ready. He scribbled on the tablet, then in one quick, clean movement, swished the plastic page up, making the marks disappear.

Pausing to watch, I wished it could be as simple and

easy as *that* to erase the wounding words and angry graffiti that Sandy and I had scribbled that morning. I did not know why it was so hard to forgive, why lifting the page and erasing the wrong from my mind—determining to no longer focus on it—required such remarkable effort. What was this need I had to be right? How important was it really to cling to my pride when compared to the happiness of a clean page?

When my husband breezed through the door on a wave of frigid air, he looked more uncertain than angry. "About this morning," he began. "I'm sor—"

"I'm sorry too!" I said. We stood together in the kitchen, clinging to each other, the faint magical swish somewhere in the room.

ᙍ

ON OUR WEDDING ANNIVERSARY last year my husband presented me with a small package wrapped in beautiful silver paper. I had hinted for a bracelet and the box was about the right size for one.

I gave Sandy a smile. Inside the box was a metal chain,

composed of three links. I don't mean three links of delicate gold chain, but the kind from the hardware store used to fasten the gate on a fence.

I could think of nothing to say. Somehow, "Thank you for this portion of chain-link fence" didn't seem appropriate. Sandy lifted it from the box. "Do you see how the two links on each end are joined in the center link?" he said. "They are separate and complete in themselves, but they share this center together. I think it's a picture of marriage at its best—two people, complete and independent in themselves, but joined in a common bond of intimacy."

The bracelet I received from him later did not affect me as much as that symbol and the meaning it carries: Relationships need the balance of autonomy and intimacy in order to remain strong.

❧

IN 1974 IN THE VILLAGE of Limuru, Kenya, I watched an elderly African woman create a carving out of ebony, a beautiful black wood. "What are you carving?" I asked.

"This is an *ujama*," she replied.

In Swahili *ujama* means "community or family." "Is it *your* family?"

"No," she said, not missing a stroke. "This is the family of Mungu." In Swahili, *Mungu* is the word for *God*.

Perhaps you would like to know what God's family looks like through her eyes? Picture a twenty-inch totem, and at the bottom, a cluster of five humans, and on top of them another cluster, and then another. They seemed to grow out of one another—their heads joined, their faces blending, this one's foot flowing from that one's hand, and all their arms wrapped around one another like vines circling a great tree.

I bought the carving and brought it home.

Sometimes I can imagine God like that African woman, carving us all out of the same beautiful piece of wood, making a universal totem where we are joined, blended, and connected, our lives inextricably intertwined.

God's *ujama*. The image shatters my illusions of separateness and peels open my heart. How can I not help but twine my arms around this vast family? How can I not know the depth of my belonging?

∾

THE HOSPITAL WAS UNUSUALLY QUIET that bleak January evening. I stood in the nurses' station on the seventh floor and glanced at the clock. It was nine o'clock.

I threw a stethoscope around my neck and headed down the corridor to see a new patient, Mr. Williams. A man who had come in alone, without any family.

As I entered, he looked up eagerly, but averted his eyes when he saw it was only me. I pressed the stethoscope over his chest and listened. Strong, slow, even beating. Just what I wanted to hear. There seemed little indication he had suffered a slight heart attack a few hours earlier.

He looked up from his bed. "Nurse, would you . . ." He hesitated, tears filling his eyes.

He brushed away a tear. "Would you call my daughter? Tell her I've had a heart attack. I live alone and she is the only family I have." His respiration suddenly sped up. I turned his nasal oxygen up to eight liters a minute. "Of course I'll call her," I said. He gripped the sheets, his face tense with urgency. "Will you call her as soon as you can?" He was breathing too fast.

"I'll call her first thing," I said, patting his shoulder. "Now you get some rest."

I flipped off the light. He closed his eyes, such young blue eyes in a fifty-something face. The room was dark except for a faint night-light under the sink. Reluctant to leave, I moved through the silence to the window. A foggy mist curled through the parking lot. Above, snow clouds quilted the night sky. I shivered.

"Nurse," he called, "could you get me a pencil and paper?"

I dug a scrap of yellow paper and a pen from my pocket and set it on the bedside table. "Thank you," he said.

I walked back to the nurses' station and sat in a squeaky swivel chair by the phone. Mr. Williams's daughter was listed on his chart as the next of kin. I got her number and dialed. Her soft voice answered.

"This is Sue Kidd, a registered nurse at the hospital. I'm calling about your father. He was admitted tonight with a slight heart attack and—"

"Oh no!" she cried, startling me. "He's not dying, is he?"

"His condition is stable at the moment."

"You can't let him die!" she said.

"He's getting the very best care."

"My father and I haven't spoken in almost a year. We had an argument on my twenty-first birthday, over my boyfriend. I left and I haven't been back. The last thing I said to him was, 'I hate you.'"

Her voice cracked and I heard her crying. I felt tears burning my eyes, too. A father and daughter, so lost to each other. Then I was thinking of my own father so many miles away. It had been so long since I'd said "I love you."

"I'm coming. I'll be there in thirty minutes," she said. Click.

I tried to busy myself with a stack of charts on the desk. I couldn't concentrate. I hurried back down the hall to Mr. Williams' room. I opened the door. He lay unmoving. There was no pulse.

"Code ninety-nine!" The alert shot through the hospital within seconds after I called the switchboard through the intercom by the bed. Mr. Williams had had a cardiac arrest.

I leveled the bed and bent over his mouth, breathing air into his lungs. I positioned my hands over his chest and compressed. One, two, three. I tried to count. At fifteen I moved back to his mouth and breathed as deeply as I could. Where was help?

Oh, God, his daughter is coming. Don't let it end this way.

The door burst open. A doctor, several nurses and a respiratory therapist poured into the room, pushing emergency equipment. The doctor took over the manual compression of the heart. A tube was inserted through the man's mouth as an airway. Nurses plunged syringes of medicine into the intravenous tubing.

I connected the heart monitor. Nothing.

"Stand back," cried a doctor. I handed him the paddles for the electrical shock to the heart. He placed them on Mr. Williams' chest. We tried over and over. But there was no response. Mr. Williams was pronounced dead.

A nurse unplugged the oxygen. The gurgling stopped. One by one they left.

How could this happen? I stood by his bed, stunned. A cold wind rattled the window, pelting the panes with snow. How could I face his daughter?

When I left the room, I saw her against the wall by a water fountain, the doctor was talking to her, gripping her elbow. Then he moved on, leaving her slumped against the wall.

I took her hand and led her into the nurses' lounge.

We sat on little green stools.

"I'm so, so sorry," I said. It was painfully inadequate.

"I never hated him," she said, staring into her lap.

Suddenly she turned toward me. "I want to see him."

I escorted her down the corridor to his room. Outside the door I squeezed her hand. We stood by his bed a moment, then she buried her face in the sheets.

I tried not to look at her, at this sad good-bye. On his bedside table I noticed the scrap of yellow paper. On it was written:

My dearest Janie,

   I forgive you. I pray you will also forgive me. I know that you love me. I love you too.

                                          Daddy

I thrust it toward her and watched her read it once, then twice.

Beyond the window a few crystal stars blinked through the blackness. A snowflake hit the window and melted away.

Life seemed as fragile as a snowflake on the window.

I crept from the room and hurried to the phone. I would call my father. I would say, "I love you."

～

AT AN OUTDOOR ART SHOW, I milled through the exhibit along the sidewalk, noticing that one painting had attracted a crowd. In the upper left and the lower right corners of the canvas the artist had painted a human heart inside a box. The rest of the canvas was blank, a gulf of empty space stretching between the two boxed hearts. The painting was titled "Relationship."

As I stood wedged among the strangers, gazing at the picture, the truth of the image pierced me. I found a bench and sat down, unable to get those boxed hearts out of my mind. I pondered the subtle ways I closed my heart and let distance grow between myself and others.

In the end, the thing that matters is opening the heart, dismantling the boxes that keep us from love.

～

ONE AFTERNOON as my husband and I lay sunning on the beach, I noticed a middle-aged couple sitting on a towel with a poodle between them. The man stroked the dog and absently gazed at the sea. The woman traced her finger in the sand from time to time, cocking her head to see the effect. Later, when I looked again, they were holding hands.

The hours passed. The tide crept away. The couple with the dog left. My husband and I dragged the children from the water and headed back to the cottage. Passing the spot where the couple had sat holding hands, I noticed the woman's sand tracing. It read, *I love you.*

I stared at the words—words I was sometimes too complacent or too busy to say, aware of how formidable they are . . . of the power of putting the feeling into words. It had caused a couple to suddenly hold hands on a crowded beach . . . and feel cherished.

In the distance the children trailed after my husband. I chased after them, my heart full of the words on the sand.

❧

ULTIMATELY, WE ARE REBORN to love because in this expanding, gracious space within us, we arrive at the astonishing presence of God at the core of our life. We blunder into the heart of God and find our own.

ACKNOWLEDGMENTS

Every attempt has been made to credit the sources of copyrighted material used in this book. If any such acknowledgment has been inadvertently omitted or miscredited, receipt of such information would be appreciated.

Introduction to *Firstlight*; "A Story-Shaped Life," "Birthing Compassion," "In the Ragged Meadow of My Soul," "Live Welcoming to All," and "The Secret of Winter Foliage" originally published in *Weavings*; "A Show of Spring" and "Essence of the South Is in the Attitude" originally published in the *Atlanta Journal-Constitution*; "Renewing My Vows" originally published in *Skirt!*; "When Noise Becomes Music," a lecture published in *Silence in the Midst of Noise*; excerpt from "Weeping with Dolphins" originally published in *Pilgrimage*; excerpt from the introduction to *Love's Hidden Blessings*; excerpt from "Severe Grace/Formation of Soul, Active Grace/ New Consciousness" originally published in *Journal of Christian Healing* are reprinted with permission from the author. Copyright © by Sue Monk Kidd. All rights reserved.

Excerpt on page 194 from *Oh, the Places You'll Go!* by Dr. Seuss, copyright TM and copyright © by Dr. Seuss Enterprises L.P. 1990. Used by permission of Random House Children's Books, a division of Random House, Inc.